PRAYERS
THAT SHIFT
ATMOSPHERES

SHIFT

TAQUETTA BAKER

BOOK SYNOPSIS

"Prayers That Shift Atmospheres" is a unique weaponry manual that provides essential keys and revelation on how to release power pack prayers that SHIFTS darkness out, and SHIFTS the eternal kingdom of God into your midst. Learn how to create heavenly atmospheres, govern atmospheres, SHIFT atmospheres, and SHIFT dimensions, while continuously living and dwelling in the momentum and advancement of God. Learn to govern and cultivate atmospheres in your home, ministry, business, region, nation, and spheres of influence. Be equipped with wisdom keys and strategies to maintain your atmospheres and establish the sustaining glory of God in the earth. Get ready to be transformed! SHIFT!

TaquettaBaker@Kingdomshifters.com
(Website) Kingdomshifters.com
Connect with Taquetta via Facebook or
YouTube

Taquetta's Bio

Taquetta Baker is the founder of Kingdom Shifters Ministries (KSM), Kingdom Shifters Empowerment Church, and Kingdom Wellness Counseling and Mentoring Center. She has authored twenty-six books and two prayer decree CD's. Taquetta has a doctorate in ministry from Rapha Deliverance University, a Master's Degree in Community Counseling with an emphasis on Marriage, Children and Family Counseling, a Bachelor's Degree in Psychology and Associates Degree in Business Administration. In addition, Taquetta has a Therapon Belief Therapist Certification from the Therapon Institute, which provides faith-based counseling training and equipping to people and ministries.

Taquetta is also gifted at empowering and assisting people with launching ministries, businesses and books and provides mentoring, counseling and vision casting through Kingdom Shifters Kingdom Wellness Program. Taquetta serves on the Board of Directors for New Day Community Ministries, Inc. of Muncie, IN. In October 2008, Taquetta graduated from the Eagles Dance Institute under Dr. Pamela Hardy and received her license in the area of liturgical dance. Before launching into her own ministry, Taquetta served at her previous church for 12 years. She was a prophet, pioneer and leader of Shekinah Expressions Dance Ministry, teacher, member of the presbytery board, and overseer of the Altar Workers Ministry. Taquetta receives mentoring and ministry covering from Bishop Jackie Green, Founder of JGM-National PrayerLife Institute (Phoenix, AZ), and was ordained as an Apostle on June 7, 2014.

Taquetta flows through the wells of warfare and worship and mantles an apostolic mandate of judging and establishing God's kingdom in people, ministries, communities, and regions. Taquetta travels in foreign missions and throughout the United States. She has mentored and established dance, altar workers, deliverance, and prophetic ministries. Taquetta ministers in the areas of fine arts, all *manners of prayer, fivefold ministry, deliverance, healing, miracles, atmospheric worship, and empowers and train people in their destiny and life's vision.*

Connect with Taquetta and KSM at <u>kingdomshifters.com</u> or via Facebook.

Foreword

"Prayers that Shift Atmospheres" by Taquetta Baker is a must read for every believer. In these last and evil days we are facing attacks, upon attacks, upon attacks in our lives, in our churches and in this world. For such a time as this, we need prayers that can **SHIFT** atmospheres. For such a time as this, we need the knowledge, wisdom and understanding on having a prayer life that pulls down EVERY STRONGHOLD. The Bible declares in *Ephesians 6:12*, *"For we wrestle not against flesh and blood, but against principalities, against powers, against the rulers of the darkness of this world, against spiritual wickedness in high places."* We must understand the battle is not a physical battle, but a spiritual battle and we need dynamic tools like this book to help, equip and prepare us with prayers that **SHIFT** Atmospheres. The word of God tells us in *2Timothy 2:15*, *Study to shew yourself approved unto God, a workman that needeth not to be ashamed, rightly dividing the word of truth."* This verse is calling on every believer to STUDY and RIGHTLY divide the word of truth. It is our job to study the word of God and spend time with Him, so we can be able to discern what is true and what is not of God. But all starts with a relationship with God.

This "war manual" will give you wisdom and detailed information on discerning different types of atmospheres that you will encounter and how to SHIFT those atmospheres. In this hour if we are not able to discern different types of atmospheres, we will allow ourselves to fall into something that is not of God. If we are not careful this false perception of truth that is being released in the earth, will become our reality, and we will fall prey to the enemy. After reading this "war manual" you will receive clear revelation and different ways on how to SHIFT Atmospheres that causes God to

RESPOND. We need God to respond to our worship and to our prayers. We are to worship Him in spirit and in truth. We should be able to see and detect *strange fire* and our prayers should be the fire distinguisher in making sure we worship and serve God and God only.

Taquetta goes into great detail in this war manual on teaching you how to recognize levels of warfare and how to deal with levels of warfare. It is imperative to know how to shoot bullseye prayers that pulverizes the kingdom of darkness. As a Kingdom Warrior who teaches about prophetic movement this is a must read for me and all who I teach because it gives step by step instructions on how to break up fallow ground before you even begin to minister in movement or in general. This "war manual" will not only help you discern and recognize demonic activity, but help you pray prayers that will cause a **SHIFT** to take place in your life, and in every place the soles of your feet tread. It is not enough to know how to pray, but you need to know what to pray when you come up against hard-pressed atmospheres. If we as believers, as ministers, as psalmists, as ministers of movement do not know how to cultivate the atmosphere how can we establish the Kingdom of God on earth? And if we are not able to establish the Kingdom of God on earth, then we are not properly prepared for battle that is at hand and that will continue to unfold against the Kingdom of God. If we not properly prepared for battle, we are walking in dark places blind, ignorant, or wondering what is going on, instead of using the God given authority He has given us to SHIFT darkness out and SHIFT his kingdom in. This "war manual" reinforces the fact that WE all are given the charge to release prayers that SHIFT atmospheres. It is our mandate to release the Kingdom of God on earth, in our cities, and in our regions. The TIME is NOW to cultivate and SHIFT atmospheres to establish God's Kingdom in your home, on our job, in your local churches, and in your community. It first starts with YOU and this "war manual" is a great tool to get you started.

You just cannot read this book, you have to study this book. It is a "war manual" that gives you tactics and strategies to break every stronghold and cultivate atmospheres where God can eternally dwell. The enemy has been trying to devour you, but I declare that as you study this manual, you shall GO FORTH AS A KINGDOM WARRIOR AND PRAY PRAYERS THAT SHIFTS ATMOSPHERES! It is time to SHIFT and SHIFTING starts with PRAYERS that SHIFTS ATMOSPHERES!

Dr. Wanda Cofield
Prophetically Spoken Ministries
www.propheticallyspokenministries.com

Endorsement

This book will definitely SHIFT not only your prayer life but your walk with the Lord all together. Taquetta has poured her heart into this well written and thought out and biblical-based book about prayers that SHIFT atmospheres. So many people have said that there is power in prayer, but I challenge that statement and say there is not just power in any old prayer, but it must be prayers that align with the word of God and that are spirit filled because anybody can pray. Muslims pray multiple times a day but the power lies in the truth of God's word and his Holy Spirit to bring it to manifestation.

With this book you are going to get an in-depth teaching that produces powerful revelation and wisdom about how you can take your prayers to the next level and begin to see amazing results in your life, land, communities, and regions. I know Taquetta and her heart for people is absolutely amazing. She is always looking to help people better understand the word of God and to help people comprehend their identity in Christ so they can rise to be the sons and daughters that God has called them to be. I highly recommend this book and I have been stirred by reading it! Get ready for your **SHIFT!**

Jenny Weaver
www.jennyweaverworships.com

Table of Contents

Chapter 1

Establishing Covenant Prayer Relationship

Effective prayer requires relationship with God, a leading of the Holy Spirit and a yielding to the presence of God. This is the reason that after people finish giving God their petitions, they do not have anything to pray. They are praying without establishing an adequate relationship, in their own will and guidance, and zap out when their needs and desires are delivered to him. This type of prayer is sufficient for a time, but true effective prayer requires the building of a relationship. It entails consistent communing with God and through the building of covenant relationship, we are guided into all truth as we learn about God and about ourselves.

> *Matthew 6:33-34 But seek ye first the kingdom of God, and his righteousness; and all these things shall be added unto you. Take therefore no thought for the morrow: for the morrow shall take thought for the things of itself. Sufficient unto the day is the evil thereof.*

Such guidance requires us to:
1. Seek first the kingdom of God
2. Seek what he is saying
3. Seek his justice
4. Release it through prayer
5. Stand in faith as we trust and expect that all he is speaking will manifest in our lives

Seek ye first the kingdom is atmospheric as it requires us to govern and live from a heavenly perspective. You pray, assert authority, and engage earth through God's viewpoint and through his kingdom. As you function from the kingdom of heaven, your identity becomes God's identity, and he begins to pray his justice and purpose through you. Your perspective

SHIFTS to ruling and not just worrying about your life and challenges. Because of your relationship with God, you learn that your life's mandate is not just to survive, but thrive, not just to live by chance but through destiny, not just to rule your life but the earth. You also learn that God is taking care of the things that concern you as you are helping him to govern the earth realm.

> **The Message Bible** *Steep your life in God-reality, God-initiative, God-provisions. Don't worry about missing out. You'll find all your everyday human concerns will be met. Give your entire attention to what God is doing right now, and don't get worked up about what may or may not happen tomorrow. God will help you deal with whatever hard things come up when the time comes.*

Exploration Questions:
1. Spend a week activating **Matthew 6:33-34** and the five guidance points above during your prayer time.
2. Ask God to give you his viewpoint for your life, challenges, and the world.
3. Practice praying what God shows you.
4. Every time you think about your life and challenges, resist worrying, trying to figure them out, or doing anything that God did not say. Instead, declare what God has said about them. Command your mind, emotions, will, body, and soul, to align with your spirit and for your spirit to maintain a heavenly perspective about them.
5. After a week, speak in tongues and ask God to download his viewpoint as you are speaking and pray what he is showing you, while also governing and maintaining your authority through your prayer language over the atmosphere. This will mature your prayer life in praying governmentally over the lives of others and publicly. Activate this point consistently until you live from a

heavenly perspective and freely receive downloads from God to release in the earth.

Chapter 2

Knowing Your Authority In God

In order to govern and SHIFT atmospheres, you must have covenant relationship with God, know your authority in God, and have clarity about who God is and is not. You must also know your identity and who God has called and destined you to be in the earth.

> *Genesis 1:28 And God blessed them, and God said unto them, Be fruitful, and multiply, and replenish the earth, and subdue it: and have dominion over the fish of the sea, and over the fowl of the air, and over every living thing that moveth upon the earth.*

Dominion is a heavenly sphere. It is a realization that you are not of this world.

> *Ephesians 2:6 And hath raised us up together, and made us sit together in heavenly places in Christ Jesus.*

After the fall of man, Jesus reestablished us in dominion. We are sitting with Jesus in a place of dominion so a relationship with him is vital to us ruling properly. It is also pivotal to knowing his rulership and how to release it in the earth.

Dominion gives you the ability to operate in the rulership of God and reign through the unique purpose he has placed inside of you. When you understand your identity through covenant relationship with Jesus Christ, then you can appreciate and cultivate the authority God has given you to be fruitful, multiply, replenish, subdue, and have dominion in the earth.

Knowing your jurisdiction will enable you to govern and SHIFT atmospheres properly. Jurisdiction is the sphere to which God has called you to reign. Jurisdiction does not limit your sphere. It enables you to determine your initial point of ruling and once you have gained authority in that area, you can expand your rulership as God leads. Though Adam and Eve were given dominion to rule the entire earth, their jurisdiction began in the garden. They did not properly govern this sphere, which caused them to get kicked out of the garden. Though they were still required to reign in the earth, their decisions in the garden caused hardship upon them and all of mankind. It also caused a contending with the adversary Satan who continuously challenges mankind's dominion and authority. Jesus had to come to restore dominion and authority where we could reign successfully in the earth. He gave us power over all the power of the enemy (*Luke 10:19*). He also made us one body with different parts so we can reign first in our jurisdiction then expand as we grow in our ability to reign (*Study 1Corinthians 12:12-27, Romans 12, Ephesians 4*).

> *1Corinthians 12:12 For as the body is one, and hath many members, and all the members of that one body, being many, are one body: so also is Christ.*

> *Romans 12:4-5 For as we have many members in one body, and all members have not the same office: So we, being many, are one body in Christ, and every one members one of another.*

> *Ephesians 4:11-13 And he gave some, apostles; and some, prophets; and some, evangelists; and some, pastors and teachers; For the perfecting of the saints, for the work of the ministry, for the edifying of the body of Christ: Till we all come in the unity of the faith, and of the knowledge of the*

Son of God, unto a perfect man, unto the measure of the stature of the fulness of Christ:

Often, we are striving to govern and SHIFT atmospheres at ministry services and events, which is definitely necessary and important to us operating in dominion. But we also must govern and SHIFT the atmospheres of our home, jobs, schools, communities, regions, nations, etc. Where is your garden???? Have you asserted dominion over it???? Do you know who you are to assert dominion over your garden???

I believe one of the reasons it has been so difficult to maintain dominion in governing and SHIFTING atmospheres in our services, is because we do not really know who we are, know our authority in God, and we have not asserted dominion in our garden. Demons have taken up dominion in our garden and postured themselves in fighting against us governing and SHIFTING atmospheres in our ministries, house of worship, and events. **I break the mistakes of Adam and Eve off of us and SHIFT us under the redemption of Jesus Christ. May you be provoked in your God-ordained identity, learning who God is, learning who you are, and ruling in dominion as you govern and SHIFT atmospheres.**

Exploration Questions:
1. Who is God? Study his character and his nature?
2. What characteristics and likenesses of God do you possess?
3. What is your true destiny and calling? If you do not know, seek God for this revelation.
4. Dominion is your place of authority. Jurisdiction is the sphere to which you reign. What is the dominion and jurisdiction God has called you to rule from in the earth? *Examples: prophet called to the church; prophet called to the nations; apostle called to the market place; teacher called to middle school children; minister called to evangelize broken*

women in poverty communities; minister called to evangelize broken women in the region.

5. What are the adversaries – principalities, powers, and territorial spirits that challenge your dominion and authority? Seek God for strategy on how to tower over and displace your adversaries.

6. Seek God for strategy on how to adequately operate in your destiny and calling so you can govern and SHIFT atmospheres where heaven manifests in your midst.

Chapter 3

Governing Atmospheres

Governing Atmospheres means you sit in heavenly places as Christ Jesus has ordained for you and you rule over the earth, spheres, climates, environments, situations, and people, from your God-given mantle, rank, and authority.

> *Genesis 1:28 And God blessed them, and God said unto them, Be fruitful, and multiply, and replenish the earth, and subdue it: and have dominion over the fish of the sea, and over the fowl of the air, and over every living thing that moveth upon the earth.*
>
> *Ephesians 2:6 And hath raised us up together, and made us sit together in heavenly places in Christ Jesus.*
>
> *Psalms 91:1 The Amplified Bible HE WHO dwells in the secret place of the Most High shall remain stable and fixed under the shadow of the Almighty [Whose power no foe can withstand].*
>
> *Psalms 91:13-14 Thou shalt tread upon the lion and adder: the young lion and the dragon shalt thou trample under feet. Because he hath set his love upon me, therefore will I deliver him: I will set him on high, because he hath known my name.*
>
> *Luke 10:19 Behold, I give unto you power to tread on serpents and scorpions, and over all the power of the enemy: and nothing shall by any means hurt you.*

When desiring to govern and shift atmospheres, we must understand that God always required that high places be dealt with. This is because nothing was supposed to be exalted above him or to cap his ability to be limitlessly, incomparably God. He is GOD - ALL SPIRIT - which means he is eternal

and infinite. High places box him in and box us into a
measure of him, his existence and our existence.

High places are physical and spiritual. They can be covens,
witchcraft businesses, and agencies, demonic temples, lodges,
brothels, demonic clubs, and stores, etc. In this case, we are
addressing pulling down these entities via prayer. We are
also speaking of high places in relations to ungodly or foolish
ideologies, witchcraft ley lines, demonic highways,
principalities and powers, demonic powers, demonic
kingdoms, ungodly political agendas, dark rulers of the
world, spiritual wickedness in high places.

> *Ephesians 6:10-12 The Amplified Bible In conclusion, be
> strong in the Lord [be empowered through your union with
> Him]; draw your strength from Him [that strength which
> His boundless might provide]. Put on God's whole armor
> [the armor of a heavy-armed soldier which God supplies],
> that you may be able successfully to stand up against [all] the
> strategies and the deceits of the devil.*

> *For we are not wrestling with flesh and blood [contending
> only with physical opponents], but against the despotisms,
> against the powers, against [the master spirits who are] the
> world rulers of this present darkness, against the spirit forces
> of wickedness in the heavenly (supernatural) sphere.*

> *2Corinthians 10:3-6 The Amplified Bible For though we
> walk (live) in the flesh, we are not carrying on our warfare
> according to the flesh and using mere human weapons.
> For the weapons of our warfare are not physical [weapons of
> flesh and blood], but they are mighty before God for the
> overthrow and destruction of strongholds,
> [Inasmuch as we] refute arguments and theories and
> reasonings and every proud and lofty thing that sets itself up
> against the [true] knowledge of God; and we lead every*

*thought and purpose away captive into the obedience of
Christ (the Messiah, the
Anointed One), Being in readiness to punish every
[insubordinate for his] disobedience, when your own
submission and obedience [as a church] are fully secured and
complete.*

We should always seek to govern, pull down, tread upon,
crush, and tower over high places. These high places can be
erected by us, people, witches, warlocks, demons, ideologists,
laws, world systems. We must govern properly so Jesus is
always exalted and we are always living and operating inside
our infinite, immeasurable, unbound authority to release and
establish Jesus and his kingdom in the earth. You will not
properly govern and SHIFT atmospheres if you do not deal
with high places.

> *Psalm 18:33 and 2Samuel 22:34 He makes my feet like
> hinds' feet, And sets me upon my high places.*
>
> *Psalm 147:5 Great is our Lord and abundant in strength;
> His understanding is infinite.*
>
> *1 Kings 8:27 But will God indeed dwell on the earth?
> Behold, heaven and the highest heaven cannot contain You,
> how much less this house which I have built!*
>
> *Psalm 113:4-6 The LORD is high above all nations; His
> glory is above the heavens. Who is like the LORD our God,
> Who is enthroned on high, Who humbles Himself to behold
> The things that are in heaven and in the earth?*
>
> *Revelation 1:8 "I am the Alpha and the Omega," says the
> Lord God, "who is and who was and who is to come, the
> Almighty."*

Jeremiah 23:24 Can a man hide himself in hiding places So I do not see him?" declares the LORD "Do I not fill the heavens and the earth?" declares the LORD.

2 Chronicles 2:6 But who is able to build a house for Him, for the heavens and the highest heavens cannot contain Him? So who am I, that I should build a house for Him, except to burn incense before Him?

2 Chronicles 6:18 But will God indeed dwell with mankind on the earth? Behold, heaven and the highest heaven cannot contain You; how much less this house which I have built.

Romans 11:33 Oh, the depth of the riches both of the wisdom and knowledge of God! How unsearchable are His judgments and unfathomable His ways!

Job 26:7-14 God stretches the northern sky over empty space and hangs the earth on nothing. He wraps the rain in his thick clouds, and the clouds don't burst with the weight. He covers the face of the moon, shrouding it with his clouds. He created the horizon when he separated the waters: he set the boundary between day and night. The foundations of heaven tremble; they shudder at his rebuke. By his power the sea grew calm. By his skill he crushed the great sea monster. His Spirit made the heavens beautiful, and his power pierced the gliding serpent. These are just the beginning of all that he does, merely a whisper of his power. Who, then, can comprehend the thunder of his power?"

Exploration Questions:
1. Ask God to identify the high places in your:
   - Life
   - Generational line
   - Ministry
   - Business

- Community
- Region
- Nation
2. Ask God for strategy on how to pull down each high place in prayer and even in the natural and implement what he says.

Chapter 4

Shifting Atmospheres

Shifting Atmospheres means you are not allowing a high place in the spirit concerning a realm you have elevated to in God, but you understand that you can go continuously higher and deeper into God, his glory, his heavenly seat, his realms, and in his kingdom.

You never plateau or become complacent, but you seek to always SHIFT higher and deeper in God and to unveil a new revelation of him, new essence of him, a new facet of his kingdom in the earth, a new essence of yourself and your own identity and mantle that represents him. You seek to reign and SHIFT higher in your authority and rank in God, to rule through God and his kingdom, encounter and literally see heaven, and release the tangible atmosphere, judgment, righteousness, goods, fruit, fruitfulness, blessings, wellness, prosperity, and purpose of heaven into earth.

> *2Corinthians 3:17-18 The Amplified Bible Now the Lord is the Spirit, and where the Spirit of the Lord is, there is liberty (emancipation from bondage, freedom). And all of us, as with unveiled face, [because we] continued to behold [in the Word of God] as in a mirror the glory of the Lord, are constantly being transfigured into His very own image in ever increasing splendor and from one degree of glory to another; [for this comes] from the Lord [Who is] the Spirit.*

> *Ephesians 1:3 New International Bible Praise be to the God and Father of our Lord Jesus Christ, who has blessed us in the heavenly realms (places, regions, origins, spheres) with every spiritual blessing in Christ.*

Notice it says HEAVENLY REALMS, not HEAVENLY REALM. That signifies that there is more than one realm we can SHIFT into or be blessed from.

1. The natural/physical realm – the earth realm - is the 1st heaven. It generally is self-focused, issue-focused, emotional, carnal, material-minded, and worldly. We should never pray from this place. *1John 2:16 New Living Bible For the world offers only a craving for physical pleasure, a craving for everything we see, and pride in our achievements and possessions. These are not from the Father, but are from this world.*

2. The sky that we can see along with the galaxies, spheres, and REALMS that we cannot see with the natural eye, is the 2nd heaven. The 2nd heaven is where principalities and powers, witches and warlocks, wicked and ignorant people who desire power and fame operate. This 2nd heaven tends to be depressed, oppressive, sullen, dark, gloomy, double-minded, uncertain, indefinite, shady, unclear, blurred in spiritual vision and sight, fuzzy, lukewarm, idolatrous, demonic, stronghold, prone to witchcraft, mixed with witchcraft and godly or spiritual truths; concealed with false truths and hidden motives. We are to govern over these realms but not pray and live in these realms. *Ephesians 6:12 New Living Bible For we are not fighting against flesh-and-blood enemies, but against evil rulers and authorities of the unseen world, against mighty powers in this dark world, and against evil spirits in the heavenly places.*

3. The kingdom of God is the 3rd heaven. The 3rd heaven has all authority over the first and the second heaven. The 3rd heaven is the HEAVENLY REALMS we are speaking about in this chapter. The 3rd heaven is pure,

holy, righteous, virtuous, just, God-focused, producing of God's report, grounded in godly truth and standards, liberated, accelerated, has the potential for acceleration and upward mobility, potent, creative, fruitful, miraculous, delivering, healing, empowering, supportive, all powerful, demonstrative, judgmental and resistant to the demonic, carnal, haughty, and worldly. The 3rd heaven has levels and dimensions we can tap into. This is an infinite realm so we can always go higher and deeper in maturity and dimensional SHIFT inside the 3rd heaven. The more we govern and operate inside the 3rd heaven, the more the spheres of these realms are unveiled to us. We should always pray from the 3rd heaven realms. *Matthew 6:9-13 After this manner therefore pray ye: Our Father which art in heaven, Hallowed be thy name. Thy kingdom come, Thy will be done in earth, as it is in heaven. Give us this day our daily bread. And forgive us our debts, as we forgive our debtors. And lead us not into temptation, but deliver us from evil: For thine is the kingdom, and the power, and the glory, forever. Amen.*

Jesus sits in heavenly realms - heavenly places and gives us wisdom and knowledge to know him, his authority, his heavenly positions, his realms, and his kingdom.

Ephesians 1:17-23 That the God of our Lord Jesus Christ, the Father of glory, may give unto you the spirit of wisdom and revelation in the knowledge of him: The eyes of your understanding being enlightened; that ye may know what is the hope of his calling, and what the riches of the glory of his inheritance in the saints, And what is the exceeding greatness of his power to us-ward who believe, according to the working of his mighty power, Which he wrought in Christ, when he raised him from the dead, and set him at his own right hand in the heavenly places, Far above all principality, and power, and might, and dominion, and every name that is named, not only in this world, but also in that which is to come. And hath put all things under his feet, and gave him to be the head over all things to the church, Which is his body, the fulness of him that filleth all in all.

God wants us to and gives us the ability to SHIFT from level to level and glory to glory in him and his spheres.

Habakkuk 3:19 The Amplified Bible The Lord God is my Strength, my personal bravery, and my invincible army; He makes my feet like hinds' feet and will make me to walk [not to stand still in terror, but to walk] and make [spiritual] progress upon my high places [of trouble, suffering, or responsibility]! For the Chief Musician; with my stringed instruments.

We increase in strength to SHIFT higher and deeper in God.

Psalms 84:7 The Amplified Bible They go from strength to strength [increasing in victorious power]; each of them appears before God in Zion.

The deeper we exalt in the heavenly realms of God, the more powerful we become in our mantle, calling, authority, kingdom substance, and with bringing heaven to earth.

Never build a high place in God. Always seek to go higher and deeper in him than your present experience or understanding in him. If he desires you to remain in that dimension, he will convey that to you. Commune with him through a daily lifestyle journey, and in every SHIFT, learn what he desires you to know and experience, so he can SHIFT you higher when he is ready to do so.

16

Exploration Questions:

1. Learn the three heavenly spheres and their characteristics.
2. Practice daily discerning what heavenly sphere you are in and being mindful to live and reign from the 3rd heavens.
3. As you learn to live and pray from the 3rd heavens, ask God when you need to SHIFT deeper and higher inside of this sphere and to teach you the mysteries, abilities, capabilities of the realms he is SHIFTING you into.

Chapter 5

Cultivating The Atmosphere Of Heaven In Your Home

Joshua **24:15** *New International Version But if serving the Lord seems undesirable to you, then choose for yourselves this day whom you will serve, whether the gods your ancestors served beyond the Euphrates, or the gods of the Amorites, in whose land you are living. But as for me and my household, we will serve the Lord.*

Often, we quote this scripture and even have it posted in our homes, but much of what is in our home demonstrates that we are Lord of our home and not God. It is important to be able to govern and SHIFT atmospheres in your personal life and then SHIFT to asserting authority in these areas over land, places, and regions.

Banner of God
Scriptures, names and characteristics of God, and kingdom words are powerful tools for establishing the name, authority, glory, and kingdom of God in your atmosphere.

> *Exodus* **17:15-16** *The Amplified Bible Moses built an altar and named it The LORD is My Banner; and he said, "The LORD has sworn; the LORD will have war against Amalek from generation to generation."*

> *Psalm* **20:5** *We will rejoice in thy salvation, and in the name of our God we will set up our banners: the Lord fulfil all thy petitions.*

> *Psalm* **60:4** *You have given a banner to those who fear You, That it may be displayed because of the truth. Selah.*

Song of Solomon 2:4 He has brought me to his banquet hall, And his banner over me is love.

Isaiah 11:10 The Amplified Bible And it shall be in that day that the Root of Jesse shall stand as a signal for the peoples; of Him shall the nations inquire and seek knowledge, and His dwelling shall be glory [His rest glorious]!

John 12:32 And I, if I am lifted up from the earth, will draw all men to Myself.

I love to use *Psalms 91* as a banner over my home. I decree it loud and boldly into the atmosphere to assert the Lord's governmental rulership over my life, family, and home.

Anointing Oil

I will not go into the significance of anointing oil and the benefits of anointing your home as that is information you can easily search via the internet. Anointing your home blesses it with the headship of Jesus Christ and establishes God's honor over it.

Genesis 28:18 And Jacob rose up early in the morning, and took the stone that he had put [for] his pillows, and set it up [for] a pillar, and poured oil upon the top of it.

When I anoint my home, I use pure olive oil or anointing oil that has been prayed over by myself or a person or ministry I trust. Sometimes I go outside and anoint the four corners of my land and around the barriers of my land. I may pour oil there or just put a few drops on the tips of my fingers and anoint these areas. I anoint some of the areas outside as the Holy Spirit leads. Especially the door posts, windows, driveways, entryways, and gates. I have cultivated such an open heaven that I sometimes anoint the entryway of the neighborhood I live in. I declare an open heaven over my entire neighborhood and that no demons can cross into it. I declare that over my home as well. I verbally decree out my address and declare NO demons can cross my land line – and that they are not allowed in my home or property. I break the powers from the principalities, powers, and territorial spirits in the region and decree they have no access to me, my home, and my neighborhood. For this reason, my home is always peaceful and even the most demonic, misbehaved, or contentious people are at peace in my home.

At least twice a month, I will walk throughout my house and as I pray, declare, praise, worship, etc., I anoint everything in my home. I anoint doorways, mirrors, plugs, beds, clothes, shoes, appliances, furniture, toys, blankets, dishes, food. I generally anoint and bless everything as I pray. I want everything to have the blessing, smell, taste, feel, sense of the Lord. I break any curses of witches and devils off of it and declare it is blessed in Jesus name. I cleanse everything of emotional baggage and instability that may have come from my day to day challenges or others visiting my home. I especially cleanse the beds, couches, and bathrooms, and airways of this as these are places of release and relaxation. The soaking presence in my home tends to pull these stressors out of people, and they sometimes can absorb in the beds, showers, or on the frequencies and airways of the home. I contend with any demonic infestations that the Holy Spirit may be highlighting, and sometimes I destroy and throw things away that the Holy Spirit is leading me to rid my house of anything that seems to have a demonic or ungodly presence to it. I do not waver in this area. I do not care how much it cost or who gave it to me; none of that is worth having a compromising item in my home that will sway the rulership of God. People are quick to say, "I am going to bring you back something from my vacation." I let them know not to buy me anything if they are going to get offended if I have to reject it or hammer it to death and trash it. Being nice and falsely honoring them is not worth the demons I have to contend with that may be attached to something that I am trying to keep just so they will not be upset with me. This is really the level of governing you should have over your home as well. If it looks like it is not of God or will usurp God, I will destroy it and trust him to bless me all the more for wanting me to prepare a place that blesses and ministers to him.

> *Exodus 25:8-9 Let them construct a sanctuary for Me, that I may dwell among them. According to all that I am going to show you, as the pattern of the tabernacle and the pattern of all its furniture, just so you shall construct it.*

Blood, Fire, Glory Hedge
Declare a bloodline around your land and your home and declare it belongs to God and all else must pass over (Exodus 12).

> *Ephesians 1:7 In Him we have redemption through His blood, the forgiveness of sins, according to the riches of His grace.*

Declare a firewall and glory cloud around and over your home, land, and/or neighborhood. While anointing my land and home with oil, I usually apply a blood, fire, and glory wall to securely hedge myself in during strong seasons of warfare or when I am in a region where there is strong oppression. This threefold hedge can be used at your ministry, place of business, hotel rooms, around regions and spheres.

> *Numbers 9:16 So it was always: the cloud covered it by day, and the appearance of fire by night.*

> *Zechariah 2:5 For I, said the LORD, will be to her a wall of fire round about, and will be the glory in the middle of her.*

Prayer Example: *Lord in the name of Jesus, I apply a blood, fire, and glory wall around my home and decree no demon, witch, warlock, witchcraft, demon power, can cross over onto my land. I decree anything that witches, wicked people, and demons would try to send against me and my home boomerangs off your threefold hedge and becomes their own sevenfold mantle of judgment and confounding. I decree my home is the region of heaven and principalities, powers, territorial spirits are off limits. I am not dictated to or governed by this world, but am established in your kingdom and under the rulership of you Jesus – You are my Lord, my Savior, my Protector, my Covering. I decree this is eternally so for me and my home. In Jesus name it is so, Amen!*

Angels (Daniel 3, Acts 12)

Partnering with the angels first begins at home. We learn the importance of divine protection in our personal prayer time with the Lord. As we assert our kingly right to have angels protect us in our personal lives, we then can be confident in partnering and releasing the angels as we govern and SHIFT atmospheres.

> *Hebrews 1:14 Are not all angels ministering spirits sent to serve those who will inherit salvation?*
>
> *Psalms 34:7 The angel of the Lord encamps around those who fear him, and he delivers them.*
>
> *2Kings 6:15-17 When the servant of the man of God got up and went out early the next morning, an army with horses and chariots had surrounded the city. "Oh no, my lord! What shall we do?" the servant asked. "Don't be afraid," the prophet answered. "Those who are with us are more than those who are with them." And Elisha prayed, "Open his eyes, Lord, so that he may see." Then the Lord opened the*

servant's eyes, and he looked and saw the hills full of horses and chariots of fire all around Elisha.

Psalms 91:11-12 *For he will command his angels concerning you to guard you in all your ways; they will lift you up in their hands, so that you will not strike your foot against a stone.*

Ask God to visibly show you the angels and to allow you to converse with them. You can also do this by faith as God encamps the angels round about us whether we are aware of them or not. Invite the angels to come live in your home and to guard your property and neighborhood. Give them assignments of how you would like for them to protect you and ask the Holy Spirit what type of protection you need so you can convey that to the angels. Everyone's protection level is different and often time's angels are assigned to us based on the anointing and calling on our lives. Many of the angels I have seen in my home look like ninjas or warriors. Some have been very huge and stand up over the house, and others have been bright glory glowing angels. I have a mandate of deliverance and warfare thus the reason for these particular angels. I always thank the angels for living in my midst as I am appreciative of their assistance in bringing protection and blessing to my life and ministry. It is my experience that they usually do not converse unless they have a message from God or they are inquiring about an assignment, but there are others who have more detailed conversations with the angels. The angels that I have seen are usually very focused on their assignment unless they are enjoying the presence of God, then they may be a bit more relaxed, so do not get offended if they do not chitchat with you. Chitchat with God and partner in ministry and protection with the angels.

Praise and Worship

Praise and worship draws on the presence of God and the kingdom of God, where your dwelling becomes his literal habitation. The more you praise and worship, the stronger the tangible presence of God's glory abides. Praise and worship dislodges the bondages, curses, and assignments of wickedness and births forth the protection, deliverance, breakthrough, and blessings of God.

> *Exodus 23:25* *Worship the Lord your God, and his blessing will be on your food and water. I will take away sickness from among you.*

> *Psalms 16:11* *Thou wilt shew me the path of life: in thy presence is fulness of joy; at thy right hand there are pleasures for evermore.*

> *Psalms 22:3* *He inhabits the praises of His people.*

> *Psalms 36:7-9* *How excellent is thy lovingkindness, O God! therefore the children of men put their trust under the shadow of thy wings. They shall be abundantly satisfied with the fatness of thy house; and thou shalt make them drink of the river of thy pleasures. For with thee is the fountain of life: in thy light shall we see light.*

> *Psalms 66:3-4* *Because your love is better than life, my lips will glorify you. I will praise you as long as I live, and in your name I will lift up my hands.*

> *Hebrews 13:15* *By him therefore let us offer the act of praise to God continually, that is, the fruit of our lips giving thanks to his name.*

> *Psalm 32:7* *You are my hiding place; you will protect me from trouble and surround me with songs of deliverance. Selah*

Zephaniah **3:17** *The LORD thy God in the midst of thee is mighty; he will save, he will rejoice over thee with joy; he will rest in his love, he will joy over thee with singing.*

Isaiah **62:4 The Good News Bible** *No longer will you be called "Forsaken," Or your land be called "The Deserted Wife." Your new name will be "God Is Pleased with Her." Your land will be called "Happily Married," Because the LORD is pleased with you And will be like a husband to your land.*

Acts **16:25-26** *About midnight Paul and Silas were praying and singing hymns to God, and the prisoners were listening to them, and suddenly there was a great earthquake, so that the foundations of the prison were shaken. And immediately all the doors were opened, and everyone's bonds were unfastened.*

Humility
There is power in humbling ourselves unto the Lord. This is rarely taught.

James **4:10** *Humble yourselves in the sight of the Lord, and he shall lift you up.*

Humble is the Hebrew word *tapeinoo¯*meaning *"abase, humiliate, bring down one's pride, depress, being low."*

Lift is *hypsoo¯*in the Greek and means:
1. to elevate (literally or figuratively
2. to lift up on high, to exalt
3. metaph.to raise to the very summit of opulence (wealth, riches, or affluence, abundance, as of resources or goods; plenty)
4. prosperity, to raise to dignity, honour, and happiness

Humility is key to SHIFTING atmospheres because it postures us inside of God's glory; it SHIFTS us inside the prosperity of the kingdom of God. As we get low in surrendering ourselves under God through praise, worship, trust, faith, vulnerability, abandonment, and a total yielding, God lifts us up to a pinnacle summit place of blessings and favor that SHIFTS us in the richness of his glorious presence.

> **The Message Bible** *Get down on your knees before the Master; it's the only way you'll get on your feet.*

Repentance

It is critical to repent for sins done on your land and in your home before you lived there and since you moved in. Repentance releases the unique grace and mercy of God which breaks any legal right the enemy has over you, your home, and land.

> **Psalms 51:1-2** *Have mercy upon me, O God, according to thy lovingkindness: according unto the multitude of thy tender mercies blot out my transgressions. Wash me throughly from mine iniquity, and cleanse me from my sin.*

The more we repent, the more the unique grace and mercy of God should manifest in our lives and situations.

> **Matthew 3:8** *Bring forth therefore fruits meet for repentance.*

> **The Amplified Bible** *So produce fruit that is consistent with repentance [demonstrating new behavior that proves a change of heart, and a conscious decision to turn away from sin].*

Repentance releases a cleansing, purity, and healing into the atmosphere and land.

> **2Chronicles 7:14** *If My people who are called by My name will humble themselves, and pray and seek My face, and turn from*

their wicked ways, then I will hear from heaven, and will forgive their sin and heal their land.

1Corinthians 1:19 *If we confess our sins, he is faithful and just and will forgive us our sins and purify us from all unrighteousness.*

Break Demonic Strongholds (Deuteronomy 28, Ephesians 6:12, Galatians 3:13-14)

➤ Cleanse your land and home of any curses, demonic spirits, and strongholds.

➤ Declare enmity between you, your home, family, land, and the principalities, powers, and territorial spirits of the region.

➤ Be cautious of what you watch on TV, what music you listen to and the conversations and activities you allow within your home. Repent quickly, even for the sins of others. Even for matters that may cause an uneasiness in your spirit and atmosphere that may not be an actual sin but did not glorify God. I am quick to repent for things I may have watched or others may have watched that are suspect or ended up being perverse, bloody, full of witchcraft or demonic. I am quick to repent and make everyone pray for conversations that may have turned into sin or offense, even things that may have been done in fun but ended in mockery, dishonor, or disrespect. I recognize that Jesus is listening because I invited him to live in my home and life, so I am easily convicted of anything that may not please him, therefore I repent quickly so any subtle door cannot be open to the enemy.

➢ Cleanse yourself, family members, guests, the home, land, and atmosphere of anything that will give a foothold to curses, demons, and strongholds (*James 4:7, Ephesians 4:27*).

➢ Close off demonic attacks that occur in your night season and dream realm. Witches, astral projectors, and demons sow tares in our bodies, souls, hearts, minds, homes, and atmospheres, as we sleep at night. Psalms 91 encourages us to abide in the secret place so we are not afraid and can be protected from the terror by night. Terrors not only instill fear, but they also sow dread to make life difficult. These dreadful night tares come to steal the fruit of God's rulership, glory, and presence resting upon your life. If they cannot overtake your open heaven, they will try to use your open heaven for their demonized activity or to contaminate it with matter that will bring gloom and doom into your life and sphere. Our portals are more fruitful and larger than that of witches and demons. Often time's witches and demons will attack the homes of saints and of ministries to gain access to the open heavens they have cultivated. Especially if these saints and ministries are doing a great work in the heavenlies, are viewed as gatekeepers of the region, and have been successful at displacing principalities, powers, and territorial spirits. They seek to steal these open heavens by sowing warfare that makes life difficult or possessing a land or home and wreaking havoc, thus running people and ministries off their land.

> *Matthew 13:25-30 But while men slept, his enemy came and sowed tares among the wheat, and went his way. But when the blade was sprung up, and brought forth fruit, then appeared the tares also. So the servants of the householder came and said unto him, Sir, didst not thou sow good seed in thy field? from*

whence then hath it tares? He said unto them, An enemy hath done this. The servants said unto him, Wilt thou then that we go and gather them up? But he said, Nay; lest while ye gather up the tares, ye root up also the wheat with them. Let both grow together until the harvest: and in the time of harvest I will say to the reapers, Gather ye together first the tares, and bind them in bundles to burn them: but gather the wheat into my barn.

This scripture refers to a natural and spiritual sleep. Saints love to pray once or twice and contend they have gained authority over the enemy. But demons constantly roam so they never take a day off. As violent saints who take the kingdom by force, we are asserting our right to govern with dominion. Operating in this posture as a lifestyle gives us authority over the enemy. When the enemy knows you are continuously seeking to live inside the abiding presence of the Lord, he will be less likely to attack you and your home.

The tares the enemy sows at night are planted amongst the good wheat, deeds, and endeavors that we do during the day. Tares look like wheat but are false, unfruitful, and harmful grain. They can contaminate the good wheat, bring confusion where we have a difficult time identifying the good wheat and kill the good wheat. It is difficult to rid your life of tares without disturbing the growth process of the good wheat. This is the reason it is important to guard your night season, dream realm and pray against tares being sown so they do not have access to your life.

When praying against tares:

- Close up night portals and gateways that would try to have access to your dream realm and atmosphere while you are sleeping.
- Close up entryways to witches, warlocks, astral projectors, and incubus and succubus demons operating in your sleep and night season. Rebuke the powers of familiar spirits, dream infiltrators, demonic agents operating in your dream realm and in and around your home as you sleep. You may have to deal with generational covenants and vows that have been made by your ancestors to witchcraft and idolatrous altars. You may have to cancel and contend against the assignments of familiar spirits who have been given charge over you and/or your family line.
- Soak yourself in the glory of God as you fall asleep; meditate upon scriptures and upon God. Cleanse yourself of stress, anger, soul issues, and anything that would give the enemy access to your dream realm, your heart, mind, and soul. Posture yourself inside the glory of God so you can be protected as you meditate upon him at night (*Psalms 1:2, Psalms 16:7, Psalms 63:6, Psalms 119, Isaiah 26:9*).
- Be mindful of the seasons your region is in and what is occurring in your region during different times of the year. Some regions experience increased murder, suicide, depression, witchcraft, etc., at particular times of the year. This can cause an increase in witchcraft and demonic attacks and worldly infiltration into the atmosphere and night season. I live in a college town. When the students return to school, lust and sexual perversion increases in my region. I am aware

of this and can guard myself, my home and atmosphere from sexual attacks in my sleep, and tares of perversion being sown as I sleep.

The bible talks about how God's spirit never sleeps or slumbers.

Psalms 121:3-4 My help cometh from the Lord, which made heaven and earth. He will not suffer thy foot to be moved: he that keepeth thee will not slumber. Behold, he that keepeth Israel shall neither slumber nor sleep.

Because we have the Holy Spirit, our body and mind sleeps, but our spirit never sleeps. We have the capacity to train our spirits to be active and proactive against tares as we rest at night. I learned how to train my spirit after being attacked constantly in my sleep and dream realm by demons and witches. I began to declare that my spirit man would be awake and active to discern witches, warlocks, astral projectors, and demons as I slept and in my dream realm. I declared that my spirit man would be offensive and counter attack or that I would awaken before any attacks. I filled my spirit man with scriptures on being God's warrior and my authority over the devil and as a governor in the earth realm. I became so skilled that the constant attacks ceased and rarely occur. You can be proactive too, especially if this is an area where the enemy constantly attacks you. Seek the Holy Spirit regarding how you are to govern over your dreams and night season and implement what he says.

- Do not allow witchcraft and idolatry in your home. God is very adamant about having no other God's before him (*Exodus 20:3-5, 1Corinthians 10:14-20, Colossians 3:5*). Witchcraft and idolatry place demonic altars in your home where your actions offer up sacrifices to demons rather than to God. It also allows demons to govern and enter space where only the Lord should be in your life. God will never share space with demons so he relents and allows demons to rule. We like to think God is still ruling, but this is our own delusion. We usually assume this because there may be a sense of peace, goodness, or favor, operating in our lives and homes. But this is not because of God. Demons will work for you as long as you sacrifice yourself to their altars. They will provide false peace, conditional favor, and goodness, fortune, etc., as long as you give them access to your life and home (*Study Deuteronomy 11*).

Exodus 23:33 They shall not live in your land, because they will make you sin against Me; for if you serve their gods, it will surely be a snare to you.

Demons snare you into a trap that lures you away from the covenant, covering, protection, salvation, and blessings of God. As you serve the enemy through the altars of your actions, your home becomes a shrine - high place for the devil. Demons want to inhabit your generations, your land, and your territory.

Genesis 28:4 May He also give you the blessing of Abraham, to you and to your descendants with you,

32

that you may possess the land of your sojournings, which God gave to Abraham.

Psalms 135:12 *And He gave their land as a heritage, A heritage to Israel His people.*

Psalms 136:22-23 *And gave their land as a heritage, For His lovingkindness is everlasting, Even a heritage to Israel His servant, For His lovingkindness is everlasting.*

Amos 9:15 *I will also plant them on their land, And they will not again be rooted out from their land Which I have given them," Says the LORD your God.*

They are after your generational inheritance, your lineage, occupancy in your community and region, and ruling the airways and portals in your sphere. Gaining access to your home enables them to snare all three areas where they can further distribute their witchcraft and wickedness. It is important to understand that your home and land are a part of your inheritance. As believers, we are to take up land and conquer territories. This is the reason many Christian realtors encourage believers to invest in land. The more land we own, the more we are able to effectively establish the kingdom of God in the earth, as whoever owns the land rules the financial wealth of the community. They are also able to have more natural and spiritual authority about what occurs in their community, environment, and atmospheres.

Joshua 1:3 *Every place that the sole of your foot shall tread upon, that have I given unto you, as I said unto Moses.*

Witches, warlocks, demons, and wealthy people understand the power of owning land and the power that comes with it. When you are able to cultivate the name, presence, and kingdom of God in your home, you establish heaven in the earth realm and take up territory for God to further advance his kingdom in your midst. He is able to use your home as a gateway for blessings, wealth, prosperity, favor, and salvation. Your home becomes a conduit for reaching the entire neighborhood and region. Thus, the same if you serve the devil so be mindful of this and yield no parts of your home to witches and demons.

In this day and age, it is important to know how to identify witchcraft. Witchcraft can be so subtle these days and appear good and godly. Study witchcraft in the bible and ask the Holy Spirit to expose witchcraft that is in your daily life and in society as a whole. Be alert and quick to reject witchcraft and from allowing anything you do, say, wear, or eat, to be a sacrifice to demonic altars.

Prayer
Interestingly, many idol worshippers have altar rooms or dedicated spaces in their home where they offer up prayers to idol gods. Some idol worshippers pray consistently and ritualistically at the same time every day, and there are some pagan religions that hire people who do nothing but offer up prayers to idol gods for them and their families. They know the power of prayer and communing and offering up sacrifices of worship unto their idol gods. As believers, we should be in constant dialog and communion with our Lord and Savior, the only true and living God.

Consistent prayer makes God tangible and gives you access to knowing him as Lord, Father, and Friend. Prayer creates a heavenly atmosphere, cultivates and establishes an open heaven over your home, releases the will, purpose and intent of the Lord in your home and life, and establishes the covenant and Lordship of God in your midst.

> *Matthew 18:20* *For where two or three are gathered together in my name, there am I in the midst of them.*

> *John 15:15* *Henceforth I call you not servants; for the servant knoweth not what his lord doeth: but I have called you friends; for all things that I have heard of my Father I have made known unto you.*

It is always great to have a prayer room or a set-aside place and time to pray, but every room in your home should be cultivated in prayer. You have access to God 24 hours a day and should be communing with him all throughout the day. The more you converse with God, the more you invite him to be Lord and invite him to have access and say so in your daily life. His voice and presence become tangible and accessible as you learn his character, nature, how he responds, how he speaks, what he likes, what he dislikes, how to engage him, what pleases him, what he thinks of you, and what he desires of you. He becomes as real and available to you as a best friend that you talk to and do life with daily. You are not questioning if he is there. You know that he is because you hang out with him every day all day, and have given him access to the intimate parts of you.

The Holy Spirit and The Weighty Glory

The Holy Spirit is the actual person of the Godhead. The weighty glory of God is his visiting or dwelling presence. You can speak things into the glory and pull out the tangible presence of God. You, however, speak directly to the Holy Spirit and develop a relationship with him in learning the nature and character of who God is and how to be guided by his voice, word, truth, standard, and presence. In the Old Testament, there were times where the physical glory would manifest in a cloud and be a covering, wonder, and guide for the people. Though the earth is full of God's glory and we still need the glory in our midst, we have the Holy Spirit that dwells inside of us who leads and guides us.

> *John 14:26 But the Comforter, which is the Holy Ghost, whom the Father will send in my name, he shall teach you all things, and bring all things to your remembrance, whatsoever I have said unto you.*

> *John 16:13 Howbeit when he, the Spirit of truth, is come, he will guide you into all truth: for he shall not speak of himself; but whatsoever he shall hear, that shall he speak: and he will shew you things to come.*

> *Exodus 13:21 And the LORD went before them by day in a pillar of a cloud, to lead them the way; and by night in a pillar of fire, to give them light; to go by day and night.*

> *Isaiah 6:3 And one cried unto another, and said, Holy, holy, holy, is the LORD of hosts: the whole earth is full of his glory.*

> *Philippians 4:19 But my God shall supply all your need according to his riches in glory by Christ Jesus.*

The glory has everything an atmosphere needs to be rich in the presence of God. The glory is absorbent so an infusion occurs when you invite the supplication of the Lord to be made evident in your midst.

The person of the Holy Spirit has a mind, will and emotions so you and your atmosphere can engage and be infused with how God thinks, feels, and his convictions.

The Holy Spirit and the glory work hand in hand to fill your life, home, family, and atmosphere with God.

Acts 7:55 But he, being full of the Holy Ghost, looked up stedfastly into heaven, and saw the glory of God, and Jesus standing on the right hand of God.

That word fill means lacking nothing, perfect. It is God's way of perfecting those things which concerns us (*Psalms 138:8*). We allow him to perfect us by inviting his glory and Holy Spirit into our lives, expecting them to dwell among and in us, preparing for his presence and person of the Holy Spirit, allowing our bodies, lives, homes, and atmosphere to be glory and Holy Spirit carriers, and being continuously renewed and enlightened in his glory and Holy Spirit.

I love spending time with the Holy Spirit as friend and asking him to teach me about God and his glory. This is vital to governing and SHIFTING atmospheres:

➢ The Holy Spirit only produces truth in us and spheres and guides us into further truth.
➢ The Holy Spirit maintains the purity of the atmosphere and keeps us in alignment with clear vision and insight in what God is truly saying and desiring.
➢ The Holy Spirit reveals the secrets of God that can be used to strategize, cover and cultivate that atmosphere.
➢ The Holy Spirit exposes the hidden things that compromise atmospheres and shifts.
➢ The Holy Spirit utilizes us as agents of heaven called to command the things of heaven on earth.
➢ Partnering with the Holy Spirit provides clear insight on what we are supposed to address as we cultivate our home, ministries, businesses, regions, spheres, and events in the government and kingdom of God.
➢ There are some things we may sense or see, but the Holy Spirit will tell us if we are to engage with those things. Holy Spirit saves us from unnecessary warfare and

hardship, and we learn to govern and SHIFT through his leading.

➤ The Holy Spirit brings guidance, clarity, precision to our prayers, decrees, and sacrifices unto the Lord.
➤ The Holy Spirit keeps us engulfed in the power of God.
➤ The Holy Spirit helps us to close realms of witchcraft and the demonic.
➤ The Holy Spirit helps us to guard the gates from demonic infiltrations that plot to steal the fruit of healing, deliverance, and breakthrough in the atmosphere.
➤ We need the Holy Spirit to SHIFT from dimension to dimension where the atmosphere does not become inconsistent or stale.
➤ We need the continual infilling and fresh fire of the Holy Spirit to sustain in the daily salvation and revival glory of the Lord.

One of the most enjoyable undertakings I engage in is cultivating unique glory atmospheres in different rooms of my home. I will play specific prayers in each room, consistently play music, scriptures, or decrees tailored to the type of atmosphere I desire. I perform a routine cleansing of that room at least twice a month or more depending on the traffic in and out of my home, to cleanse and maintain the atmosphere of that room. When people visit my home, they can tell the difference in the glory of each room and often inquire about what they are experiencing. When I know I will be having guests and they have specific needs of deliverance, healing, cannot sleep, need answers and guidance from the Lord, etc., I cultivate the guest room in the glory and atmosphere conducive to what they need breakthrough for. They generally leave my home with the God encounter they needed due to the atmosphere they have experienced as the visit becomes a place of refuge and retreat for them just as it is for me. Cultivate the glory and a relationship with Holy Spirit and watch your life, home and sphere be governed by the kingdom fruit and SHIFTS of God.

Once you have CONSISTENTLY implemented these keys to establish an open heaven and God's presence over your home, then you are ready to govern and SHIFT atmospheres in your ministry, business, community, region, and spheres of influence. Be mindful that if you have not gained ground in your home, yet attempt to govern in other areas, the enemy will wreak havoc by sending warfare against your home as it serves as an open door where he can lash out at you for the work you are doing in other spheres. Also, your home is your first mandate of ministry. Be a good steward by making sure your public ministry is representative of your private lifestyle. SHIFT!

Chapter 6

Cultivating Ministry Atmospheres

I will speak about the different prayer wells later in this book, but for now know that it will be important to learn balance in when to praise, worship, soak and rest, intercede, and war. Though you may have a preference God requires them all at their proper times. Your gift, mantle, and calling must be able to flow through the wells and identities of God. Learn balance of when to decree, prophecy, exhort, proclaim the gospel, release reverence, might, words of knowledge, revelation, counsel, understanding, and wisdom. Study the atmosphere and the power of each so you can discern when and how to tap into each well as the Holy Spirit leads.

> *Isaiah 11:2-3 The Spirit of the LORD will rest on him — the Spirit of wisdom and of understanding, the Spirit of counsel and of power, the Spirit of knowledge and of the fear of the LORD.*

Learn how to meet God in the realm, sphere, mood, and momentum he is in. This requires knowing the person of the Holy Spirit. This also requires being taught and led by him in how to encounter God, embrace God, walk in your authority, govern in your authority, operate in your mantle, and have dominion regardless of the atmospheres, climates, cultures, and demonic forces; no matter where you are, what is occurring, and what others are doing and not doing. David knew how to encounter God and SHIFT heaven to earth whether:

- In war
- In the midst of the rage and death attempts by his enemies
- In the midst of a mentally ill mad man
- In the tabernacle worship with a congregation

- In a cave
- In the midst of the religious and traditional - this occurred outdoors in a parade while ushering the ark into his nation as others looked upon him challenged, appalled and disgusted
- In sickness
- In health
- In sin and transgression

Do not be dictated by music, religious atmospheres, dull atmospheres, witchcraft, or whether others know God or know how to tap into the presence and heart of God. Practice warring, praising, and interceding to no music, slow music, and scriptures. Practice worshipping to fast music or no music.

Practice decreeing, prophesying, and standing in faith with God when there are no people around when you do not feel God, when you cannot see God moving, when your faith is tested and tried, when all you have is the word and a knowing that God never leaves or forsake you. Do not let your walk with God be dependent on feeling, or circumstances, but on the truth of who God is and the truth of what his word - the Bible - says about him.

Let your focus and life be Holy Spirit led where you lean on the Holy Spirit to direct you, not you yourself, not your own will and strength, not desires and emotions, not people, not circumstances, not systems, and not demonic forces. Practice walking daily with the Holy Spirit where he teaches you all things about Jesus, about yourself and your authority, about atmospheres and realms, and about the land and the earth.

Please understand that God will respond to the gathering of his people, but it does not mean he agrees with what is occurring.

Matthew 18:20 For where two or three are gathered together in my name, there am I in the midst of them.

John 4:23-24 But the hour cometh, and now is, when the true worshippers shall worship the Father in spirit and in truth: for the Father seeketh such to worship him. God is a Spirit: and they that worship him must worship him in spirit and in truth.

God will show up but only accepts worship that is done in spirit and in truth. When we act like offering up sinful, demonized, idolatrous, witchcraft, strange fire is pleasing to God or that he accepts it, we are lying wonders. We are not operating in truth and therefore or unable to properly connect in true worship with the Lord. This may be acceptable for those who are not saved or newly saved, but for saints who know better and who desire to govern and SHIFT atmospheres, this is unacceptable and not pleasing to God. It is essential that we learn how to discern and SHIFT unclean and ungodly atmospheres. Do not try to worship, praise, teach and preach, over the top of them or act like they are not present. You will just be stirring up flesh, emotion, and hype and allow the 1st and 2nd heaven to rule your sphere. You may be encountering God, but he still requires accountability for the strange fire that is in your midst especially if you are a fivefold officer. People appear changed or are temporarily changed, but because this is a form of godliness the false fruit will not last. You will be delivering them all over again at a future event or service.

It is your responsibility to acknowledge, judge, and deal with sin, idolatry, witchcraft, demons - the strange fire. You may have to address it publicly or congregationally, or you may have to take it upon yourself to stand proxy and deal with it.

Sometimes it is a matter of standing where you are in the service and repenting for the uncleanness and ungodliness that is present:

- Repent on behalf of the people in your midst
- Repent for what has occurred in the building you are in
- Repent for the region you are in
- Repent for the sins of the land and what has been sown in the ground and atmosphere
- Ask God to purify the people, land, and atmosphere with his blood, fire, and glory

Discerning Religious Atmospheres

Religious atmospheres have a lot of strict, manmade, doctrinal order. They have set formalities, programs, announcements, preliminary rules and regulations, and ways services should be done, leaving minimal to no room for the Holy Spirit to move and SHIFT or for God's agenda to flourish. Religious order, programs, doctrines, and man's agenda often kills any liberty, move, and SHIFTING of God that manifests in a service. Or it is carved out at a specific time, and then killed when that time is over. Many who attend this type of ministry know that time and respond accordingly with liberation, and immediately shut themselves down when that carved out time is over. There can be a mindset that if God wanted that to occur, he would have written it into the program or into the doctrine of the ministry. Moreover, hierarchy tends to drive the movement and flow of who is promoted, released and used in ministry, rather than God's will and purpose being implemented. There are strict religious rules on what is holy regarding behavior, attire, presentation, and if any of these are violated, reprimands are given so you will not disobey again.

When the Holy Spirit is allowed to have his way or when God just invades a religious service, many do not know how to embrace the freedom and often have a difficult time responding. Others may respond very emotionally and even frantically as their flesh is not used to being vulnerable to the Holy Spirit. Their praises appear as if they are experiencing an uncontrollable frenzy. Their worship may be wailing, weeping, or hollering or shock and awe. This is at times ridiculed and mocked, and the person tends to feel shame and guilt rather than empowered or encouraged to seek more freedom in the Holy Spirit. Order tends to be restored and to maintain future order, the people are continuously told that the occurrence was rare. This is done to kill any passion to desire such liberation as a norm.

Discerning Manmade Atmospheres

God Is Not In The Room Scenario 1

When the atmosphere is manmade, you want to believe God is there, and everything physical and emotional about the environment, climate, and the way the gospel is presented says God is there, but you cannot discern the TRUE presence of the Lord. The people are responding to a form of godliness but the true God is not there. The word is being preached with great fervency and revelation, but God is not there. The worship is going forth with all its smoke and mirrors, passion, and pursuit of the Lord, but God is not there. The people are exalting the platform of the leader through hype and emotionalism, or through what pacifies their flesh and desires, but the true and living God is not in the room.

> *2Timothy 3:1-7 This know also, that in the last days perilous times shall come. For men shall be lovers of their*

own selves, covetous, boasters, proud, blasphemers, disobedient to parents, unthankful, unholy, Without natural affection, trucebreakers, false accusers, incontinent, fierce, despisers of those that are good, Traitors, heady, highminded, lovers of pleasures more than lovers of God; Having a form of godliness, but denying the power thereof: from such turn away. For of this sort are they which creep into houses, and lead captive silly women laden with sins, led away with divers lusts, Ever learning, and never able to come to the knowledge of the truth.

Imagine everyone learning, receiving constant word, and revelation, but never coming into the knowledge of the truth of God. Imagine consistently going to bible study, Sunday school, workshops, conferences, Sunday services, Friday night prayer events, women's groups, men's fellowships, ever learning, ever giving of your time but never coming into the knowledge of the truth. *Form* is **morphosis** and means *"appearance, semblance, or concretely a formula, a shape, mere form, not expressing a true face of a thing."* It is possible to sit under ministry for years and not be encountering transformation because the atmosphere and vision of the ministry is a mere form of God, but not of God. This occurs due to resistance to truth and wanting the gospel presented to you in a way that pleases you, pleases the leader, yet, does not please God.

One of the facts we do not recognize is that after a while, such people and ministries are turned over to their form. This is the reason we assume these ministries and saints represent the true and living God and his doctrine. We mistake their flourishment and progression for God's blessing. And because it looks like God, we accept it as God. But God calls such a doctrine corrupt and reprobate. He regards it for what it is even if we and the people engaged in it, try to make it be him.

> *Verse 8-9* *Now as Jannes and Jambres withstood Moses, so do these also resist the truth: men of corrupt minds, reprobate concerning the faith. But they shall proceed no further: for their folly shall be manifest unto all men, as their's also was.*

Leader & Visionary Focused Scenario 2

When the atmosphere is manmade, it is usually cultivated around the leader or person in charge, and his or her vision with a little touch of God sprinkled here and there. There is a lot of proclamation about what the person has and is doing; who they have saved, who they have healed, what they have built. They give glory to God after they have glorified themselves. They expect accolades and to be treated with a high prestige of honor. They have public rules that demand honor with minimal honor of others and true exaltation of God. They tend to ridicule and rebuke others publicly and constantly remind them of their error even after they have apologized and corrected themselves. Though others are helping them to build, they do not care to share the spotlight and tend to become jealous of anyone who is honored for their part in helping to advance the vision. They deem them a threat rather than a gifted teammate sent by God. They also have hidden rules that the members do not know about until they break them. These rules are often rooted in pride that is really insecurity and is usually revealed when their ego has been bruised.

> *1Samuel 18:6-9* *Now it had happened as they were coming home, when David was returning from the slaughter of the*

Philistine, that the women had come out of all the cities of Israel, singing and dancing, to meet King Saul, with tambourines, with joy, and with musical instruments. So the women sang as they danced, and said: "Saul has slain his thousands, And David his ten thousands." Then Saul was very angry, and the saying displeased him; and he said, "They have ascribed to David ten thousands, and to me they have ascribed only thousands. Now what more can he have but the kingdom?" So Saul eyed David from that day forward.

The atmosphere tends to be very worldly and appeasing to the heart of the people rather than fully focused on pleasing God. There are a lot of activities and worldly ideas and concepts used to draw people to the leader and the ministry. Often there are excuses, reasonable dialects, and even scriptures used to justify these worldly acts. People are being drawn into the concepts and visions, but there is a lot of compromise, cycling, mixture, and sin in their walk with God and within the ministry. There is a lot of justification for being a work in progress and "we always fall short," with minimal to no plan or focus to mature in the Lord.

> **2Timothy 4:3-4** *For the time will come when people will not put up with sound doctrine. Instead, to suit their own desires, they will gather around them a great number of teachers to say what their itching ears want to hear. They will turn their ears away from the truth and turn aside to myths.*

Love & Grace Over God Scenario 3

When the atmosphere is manmade, the concept of love is overemphasized and becomes the excuse for the reasons sin is not confronted, repentance is not promoted, and demons are not cast out or acknowledged. There is a false gospel that if we just love, people will be drawn into these areas of salvation with the Lord. The atmosphere is full of superficial, emotionally charged, sensationalism that appears to possess the true love and grace of God but there is no solid foundation or substance of biblical truth. The atmosphere appears to be spiritually flourishing because it is founded upon psychological concepts and applications, and new age ideologies that have some moral and even biblical standards. People live morally correct but not biblically transformed. Sometimes these ministries are led by people who had a challenging experience in their past that has tested their biblical beliefs. They have attempted to make some sense of their experience and God; especially if the experience makes God look mean, vengeful, or heartless. Rather than deny God altogether, they form a new doctrine with some biblical truths, while implementing their own perception of how they want God to be. SIGHHHHH! The mixture gives way to psychological witchcraft, so much of the flourishment we see is mesmerization, hocus-pocus, sensationalism, psychological applications, and religious formulas at work. However, the true authentic presence and will of God is nonexistent or exist in only in a measure.

Did you know that when you work the principle of a scripture it will produce for you? There are famous and rich people that equate their fortune to consistently paying their tithes and giving to the poor. Many of these people work for the devil and have sold their souls to the devil for fame, yet they consistently tithe into ministries and give to the poor. I know people who do not go to church or truly live for the Lord who are avid tithe payers. They know the principle works so they work it. This is how many moral, psychological, and new age concepts produce positive fruit. If you do good, good does come to you. If you live a moral life and work hard at your life goals, you are bound to be viewed as a good and prosperous person. Nothing wrong with these concepts and formulas. But salvation and our covenant with God is more than just working scriptural and psychological formulas. Moreover, some of these formulas can cross biblical lines that defy God's standards for holiness, righteousness, justice, covenant, family, wellness, and godly living.

> *Proverbs 14:12 There is a way that seems right to a man, But its end is the way of death.*
>
> *Way* is ***dereḵ*** in the Hebrew and means, *"a road (as trodden); figuratively, a course of life or mode of action, custom, journey, manner, pathway, habit, of moral character."*
>
> *Provers 29:18 Where there is no vision (divine vision), the people perish: but he that keepeth the law, happy is he.*
>
> *Proverbs 30:12 There is a generation that are pure in their own eyes, and yet is not washed from their filthiness.*

One challenge discerners have, is not wanting to admit the truth about atmospheres of this nature. We are actually being mesmerized by the bewitchment of the love, growth, and prosperity. They cause us to question what we are discerning and receive what is occurring as God, when deep down we know they are not grounded in him. You will not adequately govern and SHIFT atmospheres if you do not accept truth of what God is and is not. You will SHIFT some atmospheres while leaving others hell bound.

Prosperity Over God Scenario 4

When the atmosphere is manmade, financial giving, prospering and advancing are glorified more than God.

Though these needs are important, personally necessary, essential to ministries sustaining, and are part of our kingdom wellness and inheritance, many of the tactics are rooted more in marketing schemes, worldly business themes, lottery and gambling type tactics, and false doctrines regarding sowing and reaping. There can be a constant pulling and tugging to give and different needs, stories, speeches, and gimmicks used to collect offerings. Ministries stop a move of God just to capitalize off of the vulnerable state of the people. People are manipulated into thinking they cannot receive breakthrough, healing, or miracles unless they sow a seed. There are many cases when God will beckon the people to sow. However, when ministries focus on the finances alone, the atmosphere SHIFTS into a manmade auction and probably has some roots in a man-made vision rather than a God-vision.

The prosperity gospel is not ungodly. There, however, needs to be balance in making sure God is leading the vision and the giving, and that people are being fed what is needful for their souls to be saved and matured, where they go to heaven. Otherwise, they remain in poverty and have to hustle and connive to get their needs met. Or they become rich and unbalanced, and money becomes their God.

> *Proverbs 30:7-9* *Two things have I required of thee; deny me them not before I die: Remove far from me vanity and lies: give me neither poverty nor riches; feed me with food convenient for me: Lest I be full, and deny thee, and say, Who is the Lord? or lest I be poor, and steal, and take the name of my God in vain.*

Discerning Sinful Atmospheres

2Timothy 3:1-7 This know also, that in the last days perilous times shall come. For men shall be lovers of their own selves, covetous, boasters, proud, blasphemers, disobedient to parents, unthankful, unholy, Without natural affection, trucebreakers, false accusers, incontinent, fierce, despisers of those that are good, Traitors, heady, high minded, lovers of pleasures more than lovers of God; Having a form of godliness, but denying the power thereof: from such turn away. For of this sort are they which creep into houses, and lead captive silly women laden with sins, led away with divers lusts, Ever learning, and never able to come to the knowledge of the truth.

A sinful atmosphere usually feels dirty, shameful, lustful, sensual, perverted, tainted, and grievous. It may have a stinky, unpleasant, foul, or unnatural odor. God may be there, but it may be difficult to press in or to really be transformed because it seems like a blockage is there - that blockage is sin. People may be weeping and crying out and even praising and worshipping due to being overwhelmed by God's presence, but the atmosphere continues to feel dirty and clogged because most are trying to encounter God without repentance or a turning. We think God receives dirty praise and worship, but he does not. In the Old Testament, they did not enter the gates or the courts of God without being consecrated. In the New Testament, Jesus has paved the way by dying on the cross for our sin and tearing the veil so we can boldly approach God for deliverance and healing. We still must obtain grace and mercy through repentance so that God receives our worship as an acceptable offering.

Hebrews 4:16 The Amplified Bible For we do not have a High Priest who is unable to sympathize and understand our weaknesses and temptations, but One who has been tempted [knowing exactly how it feels to be human] in every respect as we are, yet without [committing any] sin. Let us then fearlessly and confidently and boldly draw near to the throne of grace (the throne of God's unmerited favor to us sinners), that we may receive mercy [for our failures] and find grace to help in good time for every need [appropriate help and well-timed help, coming just when we need it].

Acts 3:19 Repent ye therefore, and be converted, that your sins may be blotted out, when the times of refreshing shall come from the presence of the Lord.

Discerning Witchcraft Atmospheres

The Holy Spirit is God's power at work. Witchcraft is the devil's, his worker's, and human beings power at work; regular people and SAINTS (had to make that distinction clear) work witchcraft when they yield to rebellion, sin, disobedience and divisive tactics for personal gain. Sometimes people do not even know they are operating in witchcraft or being bewitched.

Saul had no clue he was engaging in witchcraft through his stubbornness and disobedience to God.

1Samuel 15:18-23 And the Lord sent thee on a journey, and said, Go and utterly destroy the sinners the Amalekites, and fight against them until they be consumed. Wherefore then didst thou not obey the voice of the Lord, but didst fly upon the spoil, and didst evil in the sight of the Lord? And Saul said unto Samuel, Yea, I have obeyed the voice of the Lord, and have gone the way which the Lord sent me, and have brought Agag the king of Amalek, and have utterly destroyed the Amalekites. But the people took of the spoil, sheep and oxen, the chief of the things which should have been utterly destroyed, to sacrifice unto the Lord thy God in Gilgal. And Samuel said, Hath the Lord as great delight in burnt offerings and sacrifices, as in obeying the voice of the Lord? Behold, to obey is better than sacrifice, and to hearken than the fat of rams. For rebellion is as the sin of witchcraft, and stubbornness is as iniquity and idolatry. Because thou hast rejected the word of the Lord, he hath also rejected thee from being king.

The Galatians did not know they were being bewitched.

Galatians 3:1-4 *O foolish Galatians, who hath bewitched you, that ye should not obey the truth, before whose eyes Jesus Christ hath been evidently set forth, crucified among you? This only would I learn of you, Received ye the Spirit by the works of the law, or by the hearing of faith? Are ye so foolish? Having begun in the Spirit, are ye now made perfect by the flesh? Have ye suffered so many things in vain? If it be yet in vain.*

You may ask, *"How does witchcraft get in the church?" "How do saints yield to witchcraft?"* Witchcraft can be conducted through spells, hexes, vexes, going to psychics, engaging in tarot card readings, following horoscopes, participating in yoga, etc., which we will discuss later in this book. Witchcraft can also be performed through works of the flesh, ungodly acts of disobedience, sin, stubbornness, rebellion, charismatic witchcraft, emotional manipulation, emotional and sexual seduction, acts of control, using position to control and manipulate people, using issues to play on the sympathy of people, demonic prayers, self-focused or manipulative prayers, false, erred and manipulative prophecies, inciting fear through biblical teachings that bind the free will of others, releasing curses to keep or control members or due to being angry or frustrated with members, and lottery and gambling persuasive tactics utilized to get people to financially give. Some of these we may not even be aware that we are doing, especially if we add a scripture to it, have a valid spiritual reason for it, and believe it is in the best interest of the ministry, ourselves and our fellow brothers and sisters in Christ. We do not discern it because we do not check ourselves regarding witchcraft, so like Saul and the Galatians, we are blind to witchcraft operating in our lives and ministries. Whatever is in people, will radiate into the atmosphere and will be present when it is time to praise and worship God. If these sins are not repented of, whether knowingly or unknowingly we are releasing strange fire to God.

Witchcraft is idolatry, mixture, flesh, and is strange fire. A witchcraft atmosphere is usually very emotional, full of hype, built on entertainment and emotional pricking, looks and acts like God, but lacks true transformation. You may feel slimmed like a liquid or cobwebs are on you, pricked as if needles are sticking you, or you may experience tingling needle piercings throughout your body. You may become nauseous and even sick to your stomach, experience cottonmouth or dry mouth from partaking of the witchcraft in the atmosphere, or feel like something is suffocating or chocking you. You may feel confused and even know you are not experiencing God, but you are being seduced by the sound, the words being released, and how your emotions are responding to what is occurring in your midst. You may feel clouded in your mind and thoughts, mesmerized, seduced and drawn into the pleasure and thrill of the hype.

You may feel burning in your eyes or pressure in the eyes. You may have pressure around your head, have a dull, nagging, or piercing headache, feel boxed in around your head or boxed in regarding your ability to truly encounter the true and living God. This is usually because witchcraft causes a bewitching and incantations that bind and prevent you from operating outside the box or spell it has put you in. It may smell like urine, sulfur or like something is burning, burnt hair, burnt flesh, burnt animals, candles or incense, even though nothing is burning. Sometimes candles or incense may be burning but smell weird due to being used ritualistically.

You may feel confused as most everyone will be praising and worshiping but there is a check in your spirit saying this is not God. You will feel condemned, guilty, shameful, torn, critical, gloomy, outcast, unjustly judgmental, as the witchcraft is making you feel bad for judging it, and often you will ignore the conviction of the Holy Spirit that is telling you that this is not his work.

Discerning Demonic Spirits
Discerning demonic spirits will break barriers and hindrances to SHIFTING higher and deeper in God. When demonic spirits govern the people, land, atmosphere, climate, and the region, they are not going to willingly relinquish their rulership. We must confront and displace them so that there is nothing between God and us.

Demon Rankings is revelation from my book entitled, "The Great Awakening: Igniting Regional Revival."

Demon Rankings

- **Demons** are demonic forces, evil spirits or devils that possess, depress, oppress, torment, influence, or stronghold a person, place or thing. The manner in which these demonic spirits attack is as follows:

  - ❖ **Oppress** -to burden, restrain, weigh heavy upon, to put down; press down, subdue or suppress an atmosphere or the soul, heart, body of a person.

  - ❖ **Depress** – to make sad or gloomy; lower in spirits; deject, dispirit, to lower in force, vigor, activity, etc.; weaken, make dull, a person or atmosphere.

  - ❖ **Negatively influence** – cause confusion, discombobulation, double-mindedness, unexplainable weariness, tiredness or sluggardness, irritation, frustration, ungodly thoughts, thought racing within a person or atmosphere.

  - ❖ **Possess** – to occupy, dominate, or control a person or atmosphere.

- **Strongholds** are demonically possessed, demonically depressed, demonically gripping clutches, barriers, fortresses, walls, or entanglements that harass, influence, hinder and/or prevent a person from being free to walk in the full salvation of the Lord (*2Corinthians 10:3-5, Ephesians 4:22-23, Matthew 16:19, Mark 3:27*).

- **Principalities** are satanic princes and territorial spirits ruling over a nation, city, region, and community for the purposes of establishing Satan's demonic plan in people lives and spheres.

- **Powers** are high ranking supernatural demons or demonic influences that cause evil and sin in the world.

- **Rulers of Darkness** are demonic forces that govern deception and manipulative hardships and catastrophes that are generally produced by witchcraft, manipulation of the weather and worldly systems; they operate in cultures and countries such that idolatry and sin reign in the earth.

- **Spiritual Wickedness in High Places** are evil plots and deceptions, and demonic attacks directed in and against the church and God's people for the purposes of hindering, contaminating and demolishing God's will in the earth.

Determine what roots, characteristics, fruits, infestations, and workings are binding an atmosphere and ask the Holy Spirit:
- ➤ What spirits are at work?
- ➤ What demonic ranking are the spirits operating in?
- ➤ Whether it is binding the people, building, land, atmosphere, climate, community, and region.
- ➤ Strategy for casting out and/or displaying the spirits.
- ➤ Trust and use the strategies God gives you to overthrow the demons. Remember he uses the foolish weapons to confound the wise (*1Corinthians 2:27*).

If you are striving to cultivate an atmosphere, ask God to reveal to you the principalities and powers ruling that region and atmosphere so you can consistently contend against them such that you can establish an open heaven and the kingdom of God in your midst.

If you are traveling, spend time seeking God for the principalities, territorial spirits, and powers governing the region, atmosphere, land, and people you will be ministering to. Seek him for strategy to contend and overthrow these demonic entities. Be offensive by praying against them before you go on assignment and have your prayer team contend against them. Release angels into that sphere to assist you and declare the glory and kingdom of God in that sphere to cultivate an atmosphere before you even set foot on the land. God will meet you there and it will be easier to displace strongholds as you minister.

Do not build a high place by trying to manifest the same atmosphere in every service. Seek God for the type of atmosphere and breakthrough he desires for each service. Remember you are operating in REALMS OF HEAVEN so seek to go from level to level and glory to glory in God.

God may have you combat the same demonic spirits or strongholds or different ones. He may also have you bringing levels of breakthrough to the people, building, land, climate, community, and region. You may discern more demonic spirits and strongholds than God desires you to deal with. Operate at his leading so the warfare will not be unnecessarily difficult and so you are warring through his grace that unveils victory.

Discerning Godly Atmospheres
Godly atmospheres manifest the character, nature, spirit, presence, truth, creativity, fruit, power, multiplication, rulership, subduing, dominion, and kingdom of God. God is the ultimate authority, and there is no contention against his rulership or his workings. Holiness, righteousness, and purity will be evident and tangible.

> *Isaiah 6:3 And one cried unto another, and said, Holy, holy, holy, is the LORD of hosts: the whole earth is full of his glory.*

> *1Peter 1:16 Because it is written, Be ye holy; for I am holy.*

Holy is *qadosh* in he Hebrew and *hagios* in the Greek and means, *"sacred (physically, pure, morally blameless or religious, ceremonially, consecrated), most holy unto God."*

> **Psalms 145:17** *The LORD is righteous in all his ways, and holy in all his works.*

Righteous is **sadiyq** in the Hebrew and means:
1. just, lawful, righteous
2. just, righteous (in government)
3. just, right (in one's cause)
4. just, righteous (in conduct and character)
5. righteous (as justified and vindicated by God)
6. right, correct, lawful

> **Titus 1:15** *Unto the pure all things are pure: but unto them that are defiled and unbelieving is nothing pure; but even their mind and conscience is defiled.*

Pure is **katharos** in the Greek and means:
1. of uncertain affinity; clean (literally or figuratively)
2. clean, clear, pure
3. physically purified by fire in a similitude, like a vine cleansed by pruning and so fitted to bear fruit
4. in a Levitical sense clean, the use of which is not forbidden, imparts no uncleanness
5. ethically free from corrupt desire, from sin and guilt
6. free from every admixture of what is false, sincere, genuine
7. blameless, innocent, unstained with the guilt of anything

> **Philippians 4:8** *Finally, brethren, whatever is true, whatever is honorable, whatever is right, whatever is pure, whatever is lovely, whatever is of good repute, if there is any excellence and if anything worthy of praise, dwell on these things.*

The atmosphere, people, and region will become:

- God-focused
- God reverenced
- God yielded
- God exalted and glorified
- Holy Spirit led
- Pure and consecrated - not filthy, sinless or undefiled - the people recognize God is in the room so they are purifying themselves in his presence by repenting of their sins, cleansing themselves with his presence, receiving the transformation of his presence. They are not just enjoying his presence but partaking of it so they can be changed and then after being consecrated, they enjoy it.
- Just, lawful, righteousness - I believe this means that we do not just partake of his presence because we can and because it is available but we honor him enough to make sure we are in right standing with him to partake of his presence which goes back to consecrating oneself through the repentance and cleansing of sin and transgressions.

God further responds by manifesting his love, grace, mercy, deliverance, healings, liberation, miracles, signs, wonders, revelation, prophecy, knowledge, wisdom, counsel.

A true sign of a God atmosphere is whether there was transformation. Were the people, atmosphere, land, climate, community, region, and sphere transformed? It is definitely possible to encounter God and not change.

- ➤ The devil lived in heaven and was unchanged.
- ➤ Judas encountered Jesus, grew in his gifts but was unchanged in his character and ability to avoid demonic possession.
- ➤ Peter was in Jesus' inner circle and still was able to be sifted by the devil.

- ➢ Jesus ministered in some regions but could not do many miracles or fully impact them because of unbelief.
- ➢ People saw Jesus do miracles, signs, and wonders, and teach the scriptures with precision and confirmation, but they still crucified him, as they did not recognize him as the Messiah.

We have done enough church without manifesting or establishing the fullness of the kingdom of God. Now that we have an opportunity to do better, we must be intentional in being transformed and about transforming people, lands, and atmospheres. May God's sovereignty and matchless power overtake you, as you govern and SHIFT atmospheres for his glory. SHIFT!

2Corinthians 5:17 Therefore, if anyone is in Christ, he is a new creation. The old has passed away; behold, the new has come.

Ezekiel 36:26 And I will give you a new heart, and a new spirit I will put within you. And I will remove the heart of stone from your flesh and give you a heart of flesh.

Philippians 1:6 And I am sure of this, that he who began a good work in you will bring it to completion at the day of Jesus Christ.

Psalm 139:23-24 Search me, O God, and know my heart! Try me and know my thoughts! And see if there be any grievous way in me, and lead me in the way everlasting!

Jeremiah 32:38-40 And they shall be my people, and I will be their God. I will give them one heart and one way, that they may fear me forever, for their own good and the good of their children after them. I will make with them an everlasting covenant, that I will not turn away from doing good to them. And I will put the fear of me in their hearts, that they may not turn from me.

Psalms 60:2 Berean Study Bible *You have shaken the land and torn it open. Heal its fractures, for it is quaking.*

Utilize the revelation in this chapter to help you cultivate your ability to discern atmospheres. Be intentional in asking God to transform you, lands, atmospheres, climates, regions, and spheres. Ask him to be specific about the work he is doing so you can have clarity about what is occurring in you and in your midst.

Chapter 7

Praise Prayers

In the next several chapters, we will discuss prayer wells that SHIFT atmospheres. Be purposeful in learning each well so you can effectively flow in SHIFTING heaven to earth.

Praise prayers are where you use the weapon of thanksgiving and exaltation to assert authority over the atmosphere, blast devils, and give God glory. Your posture of praises of adoration and thanksgiving humbles you under the sovereignty of God, the mighty hand of God, inside the gates and courts of God and SHIFTS God into total control of being an incomparable God, contending against the enemy, and answering your prayers. Your posture in lifting him up and allowing him to get glory through his sovereignty and matchlessness, fills up the airways, the heavenlies, your life, your situations, and all that concerns you.

> *Psalm 92:13 Planted in the house of the LORD, they will flourish in the courts of our God.*
>
> *Psalms 100:4 Enter into his gates (heavenlies) with thanksgiving, and into his courts (throne room) with praise (exaltation): be thankful (adoration) unto him, and bless his name.*

As you praise, the gates of Heaven are opened to you and you are postured inside the court room - the throne room of heaven.

Gates represent access and courts represent judgment (make judicial decisions) and justice (administer deserved punishments or rewards) being released. Your praise of God and unto God is releasing and filling up your life, generations, situations, regions, spheres, nations, climates, frequencies, and airways, with the truth of who God is and the truth of his identity is releasing judgment and justice on your behalf.

The power of praise:

- SHIFTS out darkness and SHIFTS in the light of God.

- SHIFTS out bondage and SHIFTS in the liberty of God.

- SHIFTS out the will of man and demons and SHIFTS in the will, purposes and plans of God.

- SHIFTS out idolatry and mixture and SHIFTS in the sovereignty and total reverence of our only true and living God - Jesus Christ!

God becomes sovereign in every situation and sphere concerning us when we praise and since nothing can contend with his sovereignty, it has to bow and SHIFT out!

Praise prayers help you explore the greatness of God. It SHIFTS you into a place of seeking more of who he is - his identity, his dignity, his purpose, his abilities, his capabilities, his might, his power, his authority, his rulership, his majesty - GREATNESS!

> **Psalm 145:3** *Great is the LORD, and highly to be praised, And His greatness is unsearchable.*

God is without number, unfathomable, unreachable, incomprehensible, so you will always be learning and growing in and with him.

Praise causes secret and unexpected vibrations and abrupt ruptures in the earth, your life, and situations that break the bands of wickedness. The literal foundation of whatever is holding you is shaken and SHIFTED to produce deliverance and freedom on your behalf.

> *Acts 16:25-26 And at midnight Paul and Silas prayed, and sang praises unto God: and the prisoners heard them. And suddenly there was a great earthquake, so that the foundations of the prison were shaken: and immediately all the doors were opened, and every one's bands were loosed.*

> *2Chronicles 20:22 And when they began to sing and to praise, the Lord set ambushments against the children of Ammon, Moab, and mount Seir, which were come against Judah; and they were smitten.*

Notice the scripture says sets *ambushments* - not just one but multiple.

Dictionary.com defines **ambushment** as, "*an act or instance of lying concealed as to attack by surprise or to attack suddenly from a concealed position.*"

The praise caused Judah's enemies to be confused. It caused them to set ambushes among one another. They began to turn in on themselves and destroy one another rather than fighting Judah.

> *The Amplified Bible And when they began to sing and to praise, the Lord set ambushments against the men of Ammon, Moab, and Mount Seir who had come against Judah, and they were [self-] slaughtered.*

65

Verses 22-23 The Message Bible As soon as they started shouting and praising, God set ambushes against the men of Ammon, Moab, and Mount Seir as they were attacking Judah, and they all ended up dead. The Ammonites and Moabites mistakenly attacked those from Mount Seir and massacred them. Then, further confused, they went at each other, and all ended up killed.

There are spoils of war from the weapons of praise.

Verses 23-25 For the children of Ammon and Moab stood up against the inhabitants of mount Seir, utterly to slay and destroy them: and when they had made an end of the inhabitants of Seir, every one helped to destroy another. And when Judah came toward the watch tower in the wilderness, they looked unto the multitude, and, behold, they were dead bodies fallen to the earth, and none escaped. And when Jehoshaphat and his people came to take away the spoil of them, they found among them in abundance both riches with the dead bodies, and precious jewels, which they stripped off for themselves, more than they could carry away: and they were three days in gathering of the spoil, it was so much.

Whewwwwww! Praise produces spoil of abundance.

Praise causes a surge, stream, flow, waterfall, and spurt to come off of your lips. The goodness of God surges and collides with your surroundings as you profess the truth of who God is in your life. Praise causes the power of your testimony to beckon heaven to drop into earth.

Psalms 119:171-176 My lips shall utter praise, when thou hast taught me thy statutes. My tongue shall speak of thy word: for all thy commandments are righteousness. Let thine hand help me; for I have chosen thy precepts

I have longed for thy salvation, O Lord; and thy law is my delight. Let my soul live, and it shall praise thee; and let thy judgments help me. I have gone astray like a lost sheep; seek thy servant; for I do not forget thy commandments.

Psalm 42:4 *These things come to mind as I pour out my soul: how I walked with the multitude, leading the procession to the house of God, with shouts of joy and praise.*

Praise is a sacrifice unto the Lord.

Psalm 116:17-19 *I will offer to You a sacrifice of thanksgiving and call on the name of the LORD. I will pay my vows unto the Lord now in the presence of all his people, In the courts of the Lord's house, in the midst of thee, O Jerusalem. Praise ye the Lord.*

Offer is *zabah* in the Hebrew and means to slaughter, kill, offer, (do) sacrifice, slaughter in divine judgment, slay.

Praise is not done when you feel like it or when you deem it appropriate. You actually sacrifice your thoughts, feelings, and ideologies for the truth that God is always deserving of praise. When you praise, you are paying a vow that becomes an offering that slaughters with judgment anything that contends against you and God.

Praise awakens revival and restores the desolate places.

Jeremiah 33:9-13 *The Message Bible And Jerusalem will be a center of joy and praise and glory for all the countries on earth. They'll get reports on all the good I'm doing for her. They'll be in awe of the blessings I am pouring on her. "Yes, God's Message: 'You're going to look at this place, these empty and desolate towns of Judah and streets of Jerusalem, and say, "A wasteland. Unlivable. Not even a dog could live here." But the time is coming when you're going to hear laughter and celebration, marriage festivities, people exclaiming, "Thank God-of-the-Angel-Armies. He's so good! His love never quits," as they bring thank offerings into God's Temple. I'll restore everything that was lost in this land. I'll make everything as good as new.' I, God, say so.*

"God-of-the-Angel-Armies says: 'This coming desolation, unfit for even a stray dog, is once again going to become a pasture for shepherds who care for their flocks. You'll see flocks everywhere — in the mountains around the towns of the Shephelah and Negev, all over the territory of Benjamin, around Jerusalem and the towns of Judah — flocks under the care of shepherds who keep track of each sheep.' God says so.

Chapter 8

Worship Prayers

Bowing Under The Government Of God

Worship prayers posture you at the feet of Jesus where his truth prevails. It annihilates anything prideful, haughty, vain, stubborn, and contrite.

> ***John 4:23-24*** *But the hour cometh, and now is, when the true worshippers shall worship the Father in spirit and in truth: for the Father seeketh such to worship him. God is a Spirit: and they that worship him must worship him in spirit and in truth.*

<u>Worship</u> in the Greek is ***proskyneo‾*** and means:
1. to kiss, like a dog licking his master's hand.
2. to fawn or crouch to, i.e. (literally or figuratively) prostrate oneself in homage (do reverence to, adore).

God alone is to be worshipped. All else must bow to him.

> ***Exodus 20:3-5*** *Thou shalt have no other gods before me. Thou shalt not make unto thee any graven image, or any likeness of anything that is in heaven above, or that is in the earth beneath, or that is in the water under the earth. Thou shalt not bow down thyself to them, nor serve them: for I the Lord thy God am a jealous God, visiting the iniquity of the fathers upon the children unto the third and fourth generation of them that hate me.*

When you engage in worship prayers, your worship subdues everything under the truth of him being the only God worth worshipping. Anything that tries to be God in your life has to succumb to who and what he is - the only true and living God.

> *Jeremiah 10:10 But the LORD is the true God, he is the living God, and an everlasting king: at his wrath the earth shall tremble, and the nations shall not be able to abide his indignation.*

> *Romans 14:11 For it is written, As I live, saith the Lord, every knee shall bow to me, and every tongue shall confess to God.*

> *New living Bible It is written: "'As surely as I live,' says the Lord, 'every knee will bow before me; every tongue will acknowledge God.'"*

- As you kiss God's feet, witches and demonic people will have to kiss his feet.
- The devil will loose you, bow, and run because he will hate to have to worship God.
- Situations will bow and align to the sovereignty of God.
- Anything prideful and stubborn will be weakened beneath your prostrate position in God.

> *Exodus 23:25 New International Bible Worship the Lord your God, and his blessing will be on your food and water. I will take away sickness from among you.*

During my prayer time, I had a vision of many in the body of Christ standing under the covering and rulership of God but not fully submitted to the covering and government of God. Standing represented a mindset that many felt they were equal to God and wanted his protection and blessings but not his laws and standards. If we are going to be true praying worshippers that SHIFT atmospheres, we must humble ourselves not just in physical worship, but a lifestyle of worship unto the Lord.

> **James 4:10** *Humble yourselves in the presence of the Lord, and He will exalt you.*

> **Ephesians 3:14** *For this reason I bow my knees before the Father,*

> **2Kings 17:36** *But the Lord, who brought you up out of the land of Egypt with great power and a stretched out arm, him shall ye fear, and him shall ye worship, and to him shall ye do sacrifice*

> **New International Bible** *But the LORD, who brought you up from the land of Egypt with great power and with an outstretched arm, Him you shall fear, and to Him you shall bow yourselves down, and to Him you shall sacrifice.*

- ✓ Bowing is not just an act of bowing before your king.
- ✓ Bowing represents a literal surrendering, complete submission.
- ✓ Bowing displays a deep respect or deferential courtesy towards someone or something that we deem superior and that we believe is worth being superior over our lives.
- ✓ Bowing represents us submitting our lives and our rulership, our government under the hand of that

which we are bowing to - in this instance we are surrendering to the government of God.

✓ Bowing bestows and displays honor. If we bow in a physical act of honor, but our hearts are not in a place of honor where our lifestyles are truly submitted, then we have the potential to be a trader and be lukewarm and wavering in our governmental submission to our God.

When we say we are bowed to God, there is a lifestyle position that signifies that we never leave that position. In our lifestyles, we should be crouched under God, yielded completely to him.

Another word for bowing or worship is prostrate.

Dictionary.com defines *prostrate* as:
1. to cast (oneself) face down on the ground in humility, submission, or adoration
2. to lay flat, as on the ground
3. to throw down level with the ground
4. to overthrow, overcome, or reduce to helplessness
5. to reduce to physical weakness or exhaustion

This definition is interesting because if we are truly bowed underneath God, we have to overthrow our own rulership and willingly reduce ourselves to helplessness. We have to literally throw our lives on the ground - cast it down like someone or something we are fighting would or like something that we don't like. We have to look at our will as an enemy against the government of God and throw it down so that we can surrender our entire being to God. We have to deem ourselves as weak. Our physical bodies, hearts, and spirits have to live in a posture of exhaustion - where we deem our will, strength, acts, and plans fruitless without God.

John 3:30 *He must increase, but I must decrease.*

Decrease in this scripture means, *"to become inferior even in dignity, authority or popularity."*

One of the challenges we have is many of us are standing under the government of God, we say we are saved and we are under his government but we are standing up rather than bowed prostrate under his governmental rule. We are vertical rather than horizontal before him.

When we are vertical, we are saying:
- We are comparable to God
- We are on the same level as God
- We are saying we have wisdom, plans, ideas, authority that are just as great as God
- We are saying we want or deserve to be just as famous as God
- We are saying we know what's bests for our lives and even for the world

> ***Isaiah 42:8*** *I am the LORD: that is my name: and my glory will I not give to another, neither my praise to graven images.*
>
> ***Psalms 40:5*** *Many, O LORD my God, are thy wonderful works which thou hast done, and thy thoughts which are to us-ward: they cannot be reckoned up in order unto thee: if I would declare and speak of them, they are more than can be numbered.*
>
> ***Psalms 40:8*** *To whom then will you liken God? Or what likeness will you compare unto him?*

Isaiah 45:5 I am the LORD, and there is none else, there is no God beside me: I girded thee, though thou hast not known me.

Pray for a literal bowing to go forth where we are truly submitted to God; where we are not standing, but are bowed - laid flat before God.

Genesis 22:5 Abraham said to his young men, "Stay here with the donkey, and I and the lad will go over there; and we will worship and return to you."

Isaiah 66:23 And it shall be from new moon to new moon And from sabbath to sabbath, All mankind will come to bow down before Me," says the LORD.

1Kings 1:47 Moreover, the king's servants came to bless our lord King David, saying, 'May your God make the name of Solomon better than your name and his throne greater than your throne!' And the king bowed himself on the bed.

Nehemiah 9:6 You alone are the LORD You have made the heavens, The heaven of heavens with all their host, The earth and all that is on it, The seas and all that is in them You give life to all of them And the heavenly host bows down before You.

Psalm 5:7 But as for me, by Your abundant lovingkindness I will enter Your house, At Your holy temple I will bow in reverence for You.

Psalm 138:2 I will bow down toward Your holy temple And give thanks to Your name for Your lovingkindness and Your truth; For You have magnified Your word according to all Your name.

Micah 6:6 With what shall I come to the LORD And bow myself before the God on high? Shall I come to Him with burnt offerings, With yearling calves?

Zephaniah 1:5 And those who bow down on the housetops to the host of heaven, And those who bow down and swear to the LORD and yet swear by Milcom.

Zephaniah 2:11 The LORD will be terrifying to them, for He will starve all the gods of the earth; and all the coastlands of the nations will bow down to Him, everyone from his own place.

Chapter 9

Decreeing & Declaring Prayers

Decreeing means you are establishing the judgments, justices, oracles, laws, standards, will, and purposes of the Lord in people, atmospheres, lands, and in the earth.

> *Job 22:28* *Thou shalt also decree a thing, and it shall be established unto thee: and the light shall shine upon thy ways.*

> *Psalms 2:7* *- I will declare the decree: the LORD hath said unto me, Thou [art] my Son; this day have I begotten thee.*

When we decree, we are releasing a command or ordination, a formal or authoritative order of law, a court order that ordinarily can only be changed if another law is released to override it.

Generally, those that are in offices of the law and rulership make decrees. This would include kings, queens, regional or national gatekeepers, lawmakers, or those in fivefold offices. These laws and court orders are God led and are for the functions of establishing the purposes of God and advancing his kingdom. Saints can also make decrees especially if they are decreeing the biblical word, as God's written word is a decree in and of itself. God's bible can never be changed and we must adhere to what is written.

> *Proverbs 30:5-6* *Every word of God is pure: he is a shield unto them that put their trust in him. Add thou not unto his words, lest he reprove thee, and thou be found a liar.*

> *Matthew 5:18* *For truly, I say to you, until heaven and earth pass away, not an iota, not a dot, will pass from the Law until all is accomplished.*

We can therefore, release these decrees into the atmosphere and command them to be established and to manifest on our behalf. Saints can also decree the promises and prophecies of God because they are laws that will not return unto us void.

> **Numbers 23:19** *God is not a man, that he should lie; neither the son of man, that he should repent: hath he said, and shall he not do it? or hath he spoken, and shall he not make it good?*

Decrees should not be taken lightly because they cause restriction and can mean the life and freedom of those who break or dishonor the decree. We learn this in *Daniel 6* when a decree was made that anyone who bows to any God or man aside from King Darius would be thrown in the lion's den. King Darius could not undo his decree. It had to be followed through with and once it was fulfilled, a new law was established in its place. Daniel bowed to his God – the only true and living God – and was thrown in the lion's den. God sent an angel to shut the mouth of the lion which spared Daniel's life. The men who tricked King Darius into signing the decree were tossed in the lion's den and devoured.

Decrees are powerful because they provide standards and set legal laws and jurisdictions for mankind, atmospheres, lands, and against the enemy. We definitely want judgment and the purposes of God to go forth, especially against demonic forces that defy the decrees and laws of the Lord. We, however, want to be mindful that as we release decrees, that those in our midst understand what the decree is so they will not endure the consequences of violating what is being established. God does grant grace, but be mindful that a new law has to be released to override the current law. And this new law is typically only established after the original law has been fulfilled.

1Chronicles 16:24 Declare his glory among the heathen; his marvellous works among all nations.

Job 12:8 Or speak to the earth, and it shall teach thee: and the fishes of the sea shall declare unto thee.

Job 38:18 Hast thou perceived the breadth of the earth? declare if thou knowest it all.

Acts 20:27 For I have not shunned to declare unto you all the counsel of God.

Hebrews 12:2 Saying, I will declare thy name unto my brethren, in the midst of the church will I sing praise unto thee.

Declare in the scriptures means to *"announce, recount, report, scribe, proclaim, identify, give an account of, or to make known."* When we declare, we are revealing what is already ours and what is already God's. As we make this revelation known, anything that people or demons, try to claim has to be released to us. The devil, witches, and warlocks, like when we do not claim what is rightfully ours. They are quick to assert authority over it and claim it as their own. Sometimes, they hold on to what is ours for so long, that we actually believe it is theirs and that they own it. We tend to believe this about the world since God has given Satan the legal right to roam the earth, and since Satan has been biblically called the prince of the power of the air. Satan can roam and he can be the prince, but we have been given dominion in the earth. We are not subject to Satan. He is subject to us.

Luke 10:19 Behold, I give unto you power to tread on serpents and scorpions, and over all the power of the enemy: and nothing shall by any means hurt you.

We can let him know this and declare the truth of God's word such that we govern and SHIFT atmospheres and establish God's will in the earth.

Chapter 10

Warfare Prayers

Warfare prayers require a contending, displacing, and overthrowing of principalities and powers, territorial spirits, judging witches and warlocks, pulling down strongholds, demolishing high places, binding and casting out devils, breaking and nullifying demonic assignments, breaking open prison doors, and exposing and breaking the snares and traps of the enemy.

> *Ephesians 6:12 For we wrestle not against flesh and blood, but against principalities, against powers, against the rulers of the darkness of this world, against spiritual wickedness in high places.*

When governing and SHIFTING atmospheres, it is important to note that we are reclaiming what is rightfully ours. The devil is not going to hand it over willingly, but we do not have to allow him to maintain jurisdiction of our atmospheres, lands, and regions. I believe the war would become easier if we recognized that we do not have to yield to his bondage, if we SHIFT into our proper place as rulers and gatekeepers, and become offensive in towering over the enemy. With that being said, you will not govern and SHIFT atmospheres if you are not willing to assert your authority and victory over darkness. The enemy will continue to own and claim items, situations, lands, atmospheres, and realms that is your rightful inheritance as child of God. **DO YOU KNOW YOUR RIGHTS?**

Galatians 4:1-7 Now I say that the heir, as long as he is a child, does not differ at all from a slave, though he is master of all, but is under guardians and stewards until the time appointed by the father. Even so we, when we were children, were in bondage under the elements of the world. But when the fullness of the time had come, God sent forth His Son, born of a woman, born under the law, to redeem those who were under the law, that we might receive the adoption as sons. And because you are sons, God has sent forth the Spirit of His Son into your hearts, crying out, "Abba, Father!" Therefore you are no longer a slave but a son, and if a son, then an heir of God through Christ.

Romans 8:15 For ye have not received the spirit of bondage again to fear; but ye have received the Spirit of adoption, whereby we cry, Abba, Father.

Romans 8:17 And if children, then heirs; heirs of God, and joint-heirs with Christ; if so be that we suffer with him, that we may be also glorified together.

John 8:36 Therefore if the Son makes you free, you shall be free indeed.

John 14:27 Peace I leave with you, my peace I give unto you: not as the world giveth, give I unto you. Let not your heart be troubled, neither let it be afraid.

Isaiah 53:5 But he was wounded for our transgressions, he was bruised for our iniquities: the chastisement of our peace was upon him; and with his stripes we are healed.

Hebrews 4:16 Let us therefore come boldly unto the throne of grace, that we may obtain mercy, and find grace to help in time of need.

2Corinthians 2:14 Now thanks be unto God, which always causeth us to triumph in Christ, and maketh manifest the savour of his knowledge by us in every place.

2Corinthians 9:8 And God is able to make all grace abound toward you; that ye, always having all sufficiency in all things, may abound to every good work:

As a child of God – a kingdom heir – you have rights to:

Rule	Display Authority	Security	Peace
Love	Joy	Be demon free	Freedom of bondage
Fulfillment	Deliverance	Healing	Help
Needs & Desires Met	Miracles	Prosperity	Success
Kingdom Advancement	Destiny	The Throne of God	Heavenly Inheritance

You MUST know your rights and what you are asserting your authority to have, otherwise you are warring blindly against the enemy.

Often times, saints are defensive and passive against the enemy. This causes us to be wounded unnecessarily by an enemy that we should be offensive and towering over. Though warfare is a part of our journey, we do not have to succumb to it or accept it. We actually should be the one initiating and determining the battles as *Matthew 11:12* lets us know that "*And from the days of John the Baptist until now the kingdom of heaven suffereth violence, and the violent take it by force.*" Due to passivity and acceptance of battles, we let the enemy dictate the battles and we tend to enter them after he has already attacked and wreaked havoc in our lives.

Many saints receive validation of their identity and even feel a sense of empowerment through experiencing warfare. They will boast of being sick, demons attacking and following them, etc., and contend it is because of the grand assignment and calling on their life. They believe this is an indication of their anointing and their importance to the work of God. Though this merit has some truth, not being offensive or counterattacking warfare is not of God. God has never told us as Christians to succumb to the enemy. He told us that

> ➢ We have all power over the enemy (***John 10:19***).
> ➢ The enemy comes to kill, still, and destroy but we shall have life and that more abundantly through him (***John 10:10***).
> ➢ That we are more than conquers through Christ who is our strength (***Romans 8:37***).
> ➢ No weapon formed shall prosper (***Isaiah 54:7***).

None of these scriptures encourage us to be passive regarding warfare and accept the bondages and attacks of the enemy. None of these scriptures tell us to be validated by our trials with the enemy. Actually, God gave Paul a buffeting so he would not boast about his identity and calling.

> ***2Corinthians 12:7-11*** *And lest I should be exalted above measure through the abundance of the revelations, there was given to me a thorn in the flesh, the messenger of Satan to*

buffet me, lest I should be exalted above measure. For this thing I besought the Lord thrice, that it might depart from me. And he said unto me, My grace is sufficient for thee: for my strength is made perfect in weakness. Most gladly therefore will I rather glory in my infirmities, that the power of Christ may rest upon me. Therefore I take pleasure in infirmities, in reproaches, in necessities, in persecutions, in distresses for Christ's sake: for when I am weak, then am I strong.

If you are boasting in your warfare, it is probably:

- Your insecurity is exposing itself.
- Your inadequacies exposing themselves.
- You justifying your challenges with not being able to overcome sufficiently.
- Weariness and burnout with the battle so you use this stance so you do not have to fight.
- Delusion or false reality of your life and situation and what you are experiencing
- Bewitchment from the enemy to keep you bound to his oppression.
- Error teaching or doctrine.

All of these possibilities reveal wounds in your soul and identity that must be dealt with so you can be healed and be positioned to sufficiently counterattack and even be offensive against the enemy. Let's examine the buffeting of Paul.

- ➢ The demons that were sent to Paul were assigned by God so this was not the devil having open season in being able to attack Paul.
- ➢ Paul knew that specific times of buffeting would come and he knew the purpose for it.

➢ This was also not due to anything Paul did or any open doors in Paul's life. This warfare was to prevent open doors and character flaws.

➢ These buffetings did not hinder Paul from doing God's work and though they were painful and irritating, they were not distracting to him receiving revelation and knowledge.

➢ Paul was actually given a sufficient grace to deal with these attacks so he was not helpless to them and he was not bound to them. *Sufficient* in this passage of scripture means "*to avail, defend, ward off, to be possessed of unfailing strength, to raise a barrier.*" He was given the ability and power to endure the buffeting. This also kept him fortified in the character and humility of God.

➢ Paul was clear on the purpose of the warfare. A lot of us have warfare and do not have a clue what the purpose of it is, who the enemy is that is attacking us, and what we are to be learning or strengthened in because of it. Many of us do not know our calling or who we are, and are not making much impact on the world or walking in our identity and calling, yet we contend it is because of who we are and what we do in the kingdom.

My questions to you are:

1. What is in your character and even nature that God has to use the buffet of Satan to humble you? If you do not know that then you are probably unnecessarily succumbing to the oppressions of the devil.

2. Paul had the potential to be haughty but it does not say he was undoubtedly haughty. The buffet was a precaution. What character flaws do you refuse to get delivered from that the enemy is using to buffet you - you are claiming it

is legitimate warfare yet you open the door through character flaws that you need to be delivered from?

3. Is the warfare strategic to the call on your life and the knowledge and revelation God is giving you? Basically, is this revelation so enduring that you need a buffeting?

4. Who is being impacted by what God is doing in and through you? If no one is being transformed then it is probably warfare you should be overcoming but not succumbing to.

This exploration is essential to understanding what warfare is and is not, and so we can correctly deal with demonic attacks and demonic oppression that is wreaking havoc in our lives, lands, and spheres. We must stop making inadequate excuses for not being well, whole and conquering, and be delivered, healed, and empowered to tower in warfare and in our destiny journey as kingdom heirs of God. **SHIFT!**

Chapter 11

Demonic Operations

It is important to know the levels of warfare, demon rankings, and types of witchcraft that are in the world and that attack saints and ministries.   We discussed demon rankings earlier in the book, but will reiterate it again in this chapter as a refresher.

The Levels of Warfare, Demon Rankings, and Witchcraft practices is revelation from my book entitled, "The Great Awakening: Igniting Regional Revival."

Levels of Warfare

Knowing the levels of warfare reveal what type of battle you are engaging in. You do not want to be engaging principalities and powers when you should be casting demons out of people. You do not want to be casting demons out of people when you should be displacing principalities and powers. You do not want to be combating demons when you should be breaking spells.

- ❖ **Ground Level Warfare** involves casting demons out of individuals, places, and things.

- ❖ **Occult Level Warfare** involves witchcraft, idolatry, or strategic organizations that are really powers of darkness, or spiritual wickedness in high places within a community or region. Examples- Freemasonry, Sororities, Fraternities, New Age Practices, Buddhism, Tibetan, Yoga, etc.

- ❖ **Strategic Level Warfare** is where principalities and territorial spirits are assigned by Satan to directly bind, influence, and govern the activities of communities, regions, states, and nations. They also coordinate demonic activities in political, governmental, economic, financial, educational, business, and entertainment arenas.

When governing and SHIFTING atmospheres, you may have to deal with all three levels interchangeably to break the powers of darkness. Allowing the Holy Spirit to reveal the demonic bondage to you and the warfare strategy needed is key to maintaining and sustaining your cultivation of atmospheres and establishing the kingdom of heaven in your midst.

Demon Rankings

No army goes to war without studying and knowing their enemy. This is the same for saints. We must know how demons manifest, their characteristics, names, positions, rankings, and mandate. I recommend my book "**The Great Awakening: Igniting Regional Revival**," as I have chapters on the names of principalities, territorial spirits, and powers that rule regions and how they operate. *"The Demon Hit List"* book by John Eckhardt is an excellent resource for learning demonic strongholds and their characteristics. The more you study demons, the easier it will be to discern and overthrow them.

- **Demons** are demonic forces, evil spirits or devils that possess, depress, oppress, torment, influence, or stronghold a person, place or thing. The manner in which these demonic spirits attack is as follows:

  - ❖ **Oppress** -to burden, restrain, weigh heavy upon, to put down; press down, subdue or suppress an atmosphere or the soul, heart, body of a person.

88

- ❖ **Depress** – to make sad or gloomy; lower in spirits; deject, dispirit, to lower in force, vigor, activity, etc.; weaken, make dull, a person or atmosphere.

- ❖ **Negatively influence** – cause confusion, discombobulation, double mindedness, unexplainable weariness, tiredness or sluggardness, irritation, frustration, ungodly thoughts, thought racing within a person or atmosphere.

- ❖ **Possess** – to occupy, dominate, or control a person or atmosphere

- **Strongholds** are demonically possessed, demonically depressed, demonically gripping clutches, barriers, fortresses, walls, or entanglements that harass, influence, hinder and/or prevent a person from being free to walk in the full salvation for the Lord (*2Corinthians 10:3-5, Ephesians 4:22-23, Matthew 16:19, Mark 3:27*).

- **Principalities** are satanic princes and territorial spirits ruling over a nation, city, region, and community for the purposes of establishing Satan's demonic plan in people's lives and spheres.

- **Powers** are high ranking supernatural demons or demonic influences that cause evil and sin in the world.

- **Rulers of Darkness** are demonic forces that govern deception and manipulative hardships and catastrophes that are generally produced by witchcraft, manipulation of the weather and worldly systems; they operate in cultures and countries such that idolatry and sin reign in the earth.

- **Spiritual Wickedness in High Places** are evil plots and deceptions, and demonic attacks directed in and against the church and God's people for the purposes of hindering, contaminating and demolishing God's will in the earth.

Demons Attack

- **Illegally** - No legal grounds to attack but they do it because they want to control, weary, overthrow, and kill us. The bible tells us that we would be afflicted (*Psalms 34:19*) and that we would be pressed and persecuted on every side (*2Corinthians 4:8-18*). Jesus was attacked by the enemy and there was no sin ever found in him. The devil is not a legalist. He roams seeking to devour.

- **Legally** – We open the door through sin, transgressions, unresolved issues, witchcraft. Legal doors open when we are not properly hedged into God and his Lordship over our lives. It is not enough to accept God's salvation, we must submit under his protection and government as well. Otherwise, the benefits of salvation do not operate fully in our lives. They are there but we are not in position to apply them.

- **Generational Sins & Strongholds** – When sins of the forefathers have not been repented of, the enemy will use this as an opportunity to attack us. He will attack our family lines, our communities, ministries, businesses, land, regions (*Exodus 20:4-6*).

- **By Association** – Being associated with the wrong people or being in the wrong place at the wrong time can open the door to demonic attacks (*2Corinthians 6:14-18, Ephesians 5:7-11*). Sometimes people in our lives, ministries, and businesses can open the door to attacks through sin or association and we incur consequences as a result of their actions. Sometimes this can be seen as a way of bearing one another's burdens (*Galatians 6:2*). Sometimes it is just how life operates, and sometimes it is because we should have disassociated from that person but did not adhere to the warnings of the Holy Spirit. Just because the enemy uses associations as an opportunity to attack you, does not mean you have to succumb to his actions. It is important to discern where the open door is coming from so you can properly close it.

Witchcraft Practices

Witchcraft is the practice of magic, especially black magic; it is the utilization of spells and the invocation of demons to bind people, families, ministries, businesses, organizations, land, atmospheres, climates, regions, and nations. Some people engage in witchcraft for entertainment, curiosity, or due to ignorance. Those that dedicate their lives to it use it to acquire personal success and advancement, power, fame, rank in spiritual realms, spheres, and to obtain high ranking positions and platforms in the natural. People, atmospheres, lands, climates, and regions are full of witchcraft. Often, we are indirectly influenced by the actions of others. But witchcraft has to be cleansed and broken so its powers can be nullified. Overthrowing witchcraft is vital if we are going to govern and SHIFT atmospheres.

Some witchcraft practices include:

Sorcery	Magic	Witching	Wizardry
Black Magic	White Magic	Candle Magic	Spells
Hexes	Vexes	Hoodoo	Voodoo
Wicca	Mojo	Chants	Demonic Crossroads

Santeria	Yoruba Religion	Hinduism	New Age Practices
Horoscopes	Tarot Readings	Psychic Readings	Chain Letters
Familiar Spirits	Spirit Guides	High Priest/Prieste ss	Demonic Omens
Necromancy	Yoga	Shamanism	Fortune Telling
Hypnotism	Acupunctur e	Psychic Readings	Superstitio n
Reincarnation	Ouija Boards	Fengshai	Good Luck Charms
Buddhism	Tibetan	Freemasonry	Eastern Stars
Sororities/Fraterniti es	Psychic Readings	Witchery	Pagan Holidays
Chakras	Kundalini	Astrology	Tarot Cards
Numerology	Dream Catchers	Palm Readings	Fortune Cookies

There is no such thing as a good witch or good witchcraft. All witchcraft is bad and evil in nature. The Holy Spirit of God is the only good spirit. There is no such thing as a good demonic spirit. God does not desire us to use sorcery, spells, and demonic manipulation to influence anyone's life. Regardless of what perceived good, that manifests from witchcraft; its source is rooted in demonic spirits that have now become gateways and influencers in your life. These demonic spirits open doors for other demonic spirits to operate so that as bad things happen, other spirits come along and serve as perceived rescuers to keep people tied to the demonic entities. But all of this is so they can keep people as a spiritual host and gateway to them operating in the earth realm, as spirits need bodies to effectively complete their demonic assignments in the earth.

Please understand that witches, warlocks, and demons do not have people's best interest at heart. Witchcraft is rooted in self-absorbed, self-idolatrous gain, and so the witches and demons are always getting something out of it; whether that is influence, possession, demonic rank, or drawing the life source out of people into themselves for more energy, power, and strength. We must judge these workings, demonic agents, and demonic forces in our region so the people, land, and region can be delivered, healed, and set free.

It is important to note that witches and warlocks pray against ministries and leaders within their territory. They pursue information about who the gatekeepers are, and they spend countless hours sending spells, curses, and demonic assignments to hinder, stifle, and kill the word of the Lord.

Sometimes they physically visit and release curses and incantations on the people, land, atmosphere, assignments of leaders and the ministries. In addition, they will astral project into homes, ministries, and regions to release curses, spells, and demonic assignments. They will even physically war, seek to intimidate, and afflict leaders, ministries, and visions as they project themselves through spiritual portals.

Witches tend to operate during the witching hours of 12 am to 3 am. They, however, will do their work all day and night for the purpose of inciting evil upon God's people and kingdom. They are committed to their assignments. We too must be fervent in our offense in canceling these attacks before they are released.

With the rising use of social media and the online web, witches, and warlocks spiritually map and track leaders and ministries through these means. They utilize the information as manipulators to release curses, spells, and demonic assignments. We must be careful what we release online. We must also be cognizant that the web has its own set of realms and influences. It is a global sphere. We must close off and thwart the attacks and assignments that are being unleashed through these portals and gateways.

I tend to declare that witchcraft works boomerang back upon the senders' own lives, families, and camps. There are instances I will send it back seven times stronger or destroy it and their kingdom all together. God was not passive with witchcraft in the bible, and he is not passive today (*Exodus 22:18*). These entities want to kill you and destroy God's people, work, and kingdom in the earth. Holy Spirit will lead you with how to combat these attacks. The key is to deal with them. They are the main reason many visions do not come to pass, never reach full maturity, or experience the level of fruit God intended for their lives and ministries.

❖ **Incantations** Are demonic spells released around people, homes, families, property, land, atmospheres, communities, regions, or whatever the witch/warlock desires to box someone in to their control and working. Incantations can even be done around a person's mind, heart, soul, and physical body for the

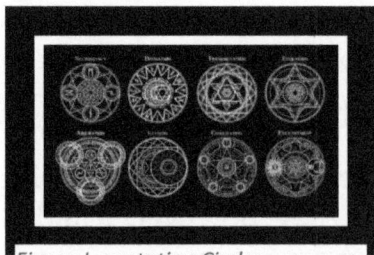
Figure Incantation Circles

purposes of manipulation and control. It will often feel like you are boxed in or something is binding or wrapped around you personally, a particular area of your body, or around the area you are in. Often on TV, it will look like a circle, but this circle boxes you in where you are bound and cannot operate in your own strength or will, or the strength and will of God. Break the powers of the demonic circle/box and command it to loose whatever it has boxed in. Loose the blood of Jesus and fire of God to be a hedge of protection around the person, land, region, etc.

❖ **Ley Lines** are spiritual lines witches and warlocks create with magic powers to hex people, land, and regions. They will release a line that has a spell on it and will place it somewhere that they know you will cross, such as a door, entryway, etc., and when you do, it activates the spell in your life. Witches are known for putting little trinkets, salt lines, cursed bibles and artifacts on the doors of minister's houses and ministries, and when they connect with them or cross those lines, it activates a spell in their life. Be mindful of this as when you begin to release regional revival, the witches and warlocks will be engaging in all kinds of attacks to bind you, weaken you, and weary you in an effort to get you to abort your assignment.

Witches and warlocks also use ley lines to communicate psychic and telepathic information to whomever they desire to communicate with; whether that be with a person they want to control or with another witch or warlock. This is how we are sometimes hit with psychological warfare. A ley line has been laid in the spirit realm from a witch to us. Break the spell and use the blood of Jesus to dissolve the ley line.

❖ **Demonic Crossroads & Spirits Of The Crossroads** are when witches work with ruler demons or demonic agents to lock down an area or territory so that only demonic activity occurs there. For example, there may be a section of the highway in your region where accidents and fatalities always occur. There may be an intercession or store where something bad always happens. That is an indication that the spirits of the crossroads are in operation.

Witches will also use the prince of the power of the air (ruling principality) over a region to bind the region to its control. They do this by going to the center of that community or region and praying a cross type ley line over the top of the city. They place an incantation around the city, and they offer sacrifices to idols throughout the year, as payment for those demons keeping their crossroads and incantations secure over that region. As a regional revivalist, you need to be mindful of this and break its power, while placing the city under your jurisdiction as gatekeeper of God and his kingdom.

❖ **Psychological Warfare & Psychic Powers** Witches and warlocks pray and release spells against ministers and ministries, especially those that are called to truly impact the spiritual and economical climate of a region. They send floods of psychological warfare to bind, confuse, discombobulate, and clog the mind, where the person becomes anxious, weary, insecure, and depressed and eventually question completing the work of the Lord. Sometimes territorial spirits and principalities use negative words and word curses that have been spoken against ministers and ministries by other people to cause psychological warfare. These words are lodged on the frequencies and airways within the spirit realm. We must understand that words have life and unless you cancel them, they live in the spirit. The territorial spirits and principalities will open the airways, so you can hear what has been said or they will use psychic powers to direct them at you, so you can hear what is being said and will begin to doubt yourself and question God regarding your destiny and calling. Because some of the voices are familiar to us and some of the voices are even things we have spoken about ourselves, we tend to take them on as our truth. Doing this binds the words to us and gives them power to further bind and discourage our lives.

Learn to discern if the floods of words are coming from your inner man or outside forces and deal with them accordingly. If they are coming from your inner man, then there is some inner healing in your soul, heart, and mind that needs to occur. If they are coming from witches, warlocks, territorial spirits and powers then,

- o Cleanse all negative words that are lingering on the frequencies and airways, and in the spiritual realm about you.
- o This is your region so command your region to rebuke, reject, and snuff out any negative words ever spoken about you.
- o Repent for any words you have spoken about yourself or others; cleanse them out of the airways as well.
- o Silence any psychic portals that have been opened so that these demonic powers cannot attack you.
- o Break the powers of word curses, verbally decree blessings, promises, and prophecies God has spoken regarding your destiny, and command them to live on the airways.

❖ **Conjuration** is utilizing the dead, demonic spirits, demonic influences, witchcraft, magic, and curses to produce supernatural effects. A lot of this occurs in regions. Especially in regions where there are huge or decent size bodies of waters. A lot of demonic activities occur under the waters, which result in spirits of the dead and other demonic spirits maneuvering in and out of the region. Ask the Holy Spirit to give you revelation of this so you can be enlightened on how to combat these entities and cast them out of your region.

Chapter 12

Offensive Warfare Weapons & Strategies

Word of God Hebrews 4:12 *For the word of God is quick, and powerful, and sharper than any twoedged sword, piercing even to the dividing asunder of soul and spirit, and of the joints and marrow, and is a discerner of the thoughts and intents of the heart.*

Bind and Loose *Matthew 18:18 Verily I say unto you, Whatsoever ye shall bind on earth shall be bound in heaven: and whatsoever ye shall loose on earth shall be loosed in heaven.*

Cast Out *Matthew 10:8 Heal the sick, cleanse the lepers, raise the dead, cast out devils: freely ye have received, freely give.*

Pull Down, Cast Down, & Overthrow *2Corinthians 10:3-6 The Amplified Bible For though we walk (live) in the flesh, we are not carrying on our warfare according to the flesh and using mere human weapons. For the weapons of our warfare are not physical [weapons of flesh and blood], but they are mighty before God for the overthrow and destruction of strongholds, [Inasmuch as we] refute arguments and theories and reasonings and every proud and lofty thing that sets itself up against the [true] knowledge of God; and we lead every thought and purpose away captive into the obedience of Christ (the Messiah, the Anointed One), Being in readiness to punish every [insubordinate for his] disobedience, when your own submission and obedience [as a church] are fully secured and complete.*

Displace *John 1:5 The light shines in the darkness, and the darkness has not overcome it.*

Tread *Luke 10:19 Behold, I give unto you power to tread on serpents and scorpions, and over all the power of the enemy: and nothing shall by any means hurt you.*

The Blood of Jesus *Ephesians 1:7 In Him we have redemption through His blood, the forgiveness of sins, according to the riches of His grace.* Passover story in ***Exodus 12***.

The Name of Jesus *John 14:13-14 And whatsoever ye shall ask in my name, that will I do, that the Father may be glorified in the Son. If ye shall ask any thing in my name, I will do it.* ***Philippians 2:9-11*** *Wherefore God also hath highly exalted him, and given him a name which is above every name: That at the name of Jesus every knee should bow, of things in heaven, and things in earth, and things under the earth; And that every tongue should confess that Jesus Christ is Lord, to the glory of God the Father.*

Our Identity – Being God's Warclub – Battle Axe *Jeremiah 51:20 You are my war club, my weapon for battle – with you I shatter nations, with you I destroy kingdoms.* ***New Living Bible*** *You are my battle-ax and sword, says the LORD. With you I will shatter nations and destroy many kingdoms.*

Angels of The Lord *Psalm 34:7 The angel of the Lord encamps around those who fear him, and delivers them.* ***Psalms 103*** *Bless the LORD, you His angels, Mighty in strength, who perform His word, Obeying the voice of His word!* ***Psalms 91***

Fire of God *Hebrews 12:27-29 And this word, Yet once more, signifieth the removing of those things that are shaken, as of things that are made, that those things which cannot be shaken may remain. Wherefore we receiving a kingdom which cannot be moved, let us have grace, whereby we may serve God acceptably with reverence and godly fear: For our God is a consuming fire.*

Hammer of God *Jeremiah 23:29 Is not My word like fire?" declares the LORD, "and like a hammer which shatters a rock?*

Strong Arm of The Lord *Psalms 118:16 The strong right arm of the LORD is raised in triumph. The strong right arm of the LORD has done glorious things!*

Strength of The Lord *Psalms 18:32 It is God that girdeth me with strength, and maketh my way perfect.* **Psalm 18:39** *You armed with strength for battle; you humbled my adversaries before me.*

Glory of God *Psalms 84:11 For the LORD God is a sun and shield: the LORD will give grace and glory: no good thing will he withhold from them that walk uprightly.*

Power of the Lord *Psalms 34:1-4 O LORD, oppose those who oppose me. Fight those who fight against me. 2 Put on your armor, and take up your shield. Prepare for battle, and come to my aid. 3 Lift up your spear and javelin against those who pursue me. Let me hear you say, "I will give you victory!"* **Psalms 54:1** *Come with great power, O God, and rescue me! Defend me with your might.*

Bombs, Hailstones & Fire *Psalms 18:13 The LORD also thundered in the heavens, and the Highest gave his voice; hail stones and coals of fire.*

Testify of Jesus *Revelation 12:11 And they overcame him by the blood of the Lamb, and by the word of their testimony.*

Confuse & Confound *Psalms 55:9 New Living Bible Lord, confuse the wicked, confound their words, for I see violence and strife in the city.*

Scatter The Enemy *Psalms 68:1 To the chief Musician, A Psalm or Song of David. Let God arise, let his enemies be scattered: let them also that hate him flee before him.*

Laugh To Derision *Psalms 2:4 He that sitteth in the heavens shall laugh: the Lord shall have them in derision.*

Wrath of God *Revelations 14:10 The same shall drink of the wine of the wrath of God, which is poured out without mixture into the cup of his indignation; and he shall be tormented with fire and brimstone in the presence of the holy angels, and in the presence of the Lamb.*

Indignation & Anger of The Lord *Nahum 1:6 Who can stand before His indignation? Who can endure the burning of His anger? His wrath is poured out like fire And the rocks are broken up by Him.*

Execute Vengeance & Judgment *Psalms 149:6-9 Let the high praises of God be in their mouth, and a two-edged sword in their hand; To execute vengeance upon the heathen, and punishments upon the people; To bind their kings with chains, and their nobles with fetters of iron; To execute upon them the judgment written: this honour have all his saints. Praise ye the Lord.*

Lift Up The Standard of The Lord *Isaiah 59:19 So shall they fear the name of the Lord from the west, and his glory from the rising of the sun. When the enemy shall come in like a flood, the Spirit of the Lord shall lift up a standard against him.*

Rebuke *Luke 4:35 But Jesus rebuked him, saying, "Be quiet and come out of him!" And when the demon had thrown him down in the midst of the people, he came out of him without doing him any harm.*

Resist The Enemy *James 4:7 Submit therefore to God. Resist the devil and he will flee from you.*

Forbid The Enemy *Joshua 10:19 but do not stay there yourselves; pursue your enemies and attack them in the rear. Do not allow them to enter their cities, for the LORD your God has delivered them into your hand.*
Warring Hands *Psalms 18:33-50 The Amplified Bible He makes my feet like hinds' feet [able to stand firmly or make progress on the*

dangerous heights of testing and trouble]; He sets me securely upon my high places. He teaches my hands to war, so that my arms can bend a bow of bronze.

Double Sword Smiting Clap *Ezekiel 21:14 You therefore, son of man, prophesy and clap your hands together; and let the sword be doubled the third time, the sword for the slain. It is the sword for the great one slain, which surrounds them. Ezekiel 21:17 I will also clap My hands together, and I will appease My wrath; I, the LORD, have spoken.*

Release The Finger of God *Luke 11:20 But if I cast out demons by the finger of God, then the kingdom of God has come upon you*

Spirit of God *Matthew 12:28 But if I cast out demons by the Spirit of God, then the kingdom of God has come upon you.*

Arrows of God *Psalms 7:13 He has also prepared for Himself deadly weapons; He makes His arrows fiery shafts. Psalms 18:4 He sent out His arrows, and scattered them, And lightning flashes in abundance, and routed them. Psalms 144:6 Flash forth lightning and scatter them; Send out Your arrows and confuse them.*

Cups of Wrath *Revelation 14:10 he also will drink of the wine of the wrath of God, which is mixed in full strength in the cup of His anger; and he will be tormented with fire and brimstone in the presence of the holy angels and in the presence of the Lamb.*

Bread of Adversity – Water of Affliction *Isaiah 30:20 And though the Lord give you the bread of adversity, and the water of affliction, yet shall not thy teachers be removed into a corner any more, but thine eyes shall see thy teachers.*

Blast The Enemy *Job 4:9 By the blast of God they perish, and by the breath of his nostrils are they consumed. Psalms 18:15 Then the channels of waters were seen, and the foundations of the world were* discovered at thy rebuke, O LORD, at the blast of the breath of thy nostrils.

Blast Through The Enemy *Psalms 18:29 For by thee I have run through a troop; and by my God have I leaped over a wall.*

Blind The Enemy *2Kings 6:18 And when they came down to him, Elisha prayed unto the LORD, and said, Smite this people, I pray thee, with blindness. And he smote them with blindness according to the word of Elisha.*

Siege The Enemy *Ezekiel 4:2-3 And lay siege against it, and build a fort against it, and cast a mount against it; set the camp also against it, and set battering rams against it round about. Moreover take thou unto thee an iron pan, and set it for a wall of iron between thee and the city: and set thy face against it, and it shall be besieged, and thou shalt lay siege against it. This shall be a sign to the house of Israel.*

Shut Up The Gates of Hell *Matthew 16:18 And I tell you, you are Peter, and on this rock[a] I will build my church, and the gates of hell shall not prevail against it.*

Cause The Enemy To Self-Destruct *2Chronicles 20:22 And when they began to sing and to praise, the LORD set ambushments against the children of Ammon, Moab, and mount Seir, which were come against Judah; and they were smitten.*

Destroy The Enemy *Psalms 143:2 And of thy mercy cut off mine enemies, and destroy all them that afflict my soul: for I am thy servant.* **Psalms 52:5** *Surely God will bring you down to everlasting ruin; He will snatch you up and tear you away from your tent; He will uproot you from the land of the living. Selah.* **Psalms 54:5** *He will reward my enemies with evil. In Your faithfulness, destroy them.*

Crush & Annihilate The Enemy *Romans 16:20 The God of peace will soon crush Satan under your feet. The grace of our Lord Jesus be with you.*

Chapter 13

Dismantling Brass Heavens

This chapter is from my book entitled, "The Great Awakening; Igniting Regional Revival." You will have to know how to dismantle brass heavens *if* you are going to govern and SHIFT atmospheres.

> **Deuteronomy 28:23** *And thy heaven that is over thy head shall be brass, and the earth that is under thee shall be iron.*

Brass is *hset* in the Hebrew and means:
1. copper, steal, bronze, metal
2. filthiness, lust, harlotry
3. dubious (of doubtful quality or propriety)
4. of uncertain outcome, wavering or hesitating in opinion

> **Haggai 1:10** *Therefore the heaven over you is stayed from dew, and the earth is stayed from her fruit.*

> **1Kings 17:1** *Now Elijah the Tishbite, who was of the settlers of Gilead, said to Ahab, "As the LORD, the God of Israel lives, before whom I stand, surely there shall be neither dew nor rain these years, except by my word."*

When the heavens are stayed or void of dew, it is:

Restricted	Prohibited	Reframed	Shut up
Held back	Forbidden	Withheld	Finished
A Drought	Famine	Dying of Crops	No Life or Reviving

There can be various reasons for a stayed or brass heaven. Some of these I will address, and some of them are self-explanatory or will be examined in other areas of the book.

➤ Sin, transgressions, and generational curses.

➤ Judgment from God due to sin.

➤ Principalities, powers, and territorial spirits ruling the heavenlies.

➤ Lack of revelation, honor, and relationship with Jesus and the Holy Spirit.

➤ Witchcraft prayers and spells, binding the crossroads of the regions. Witches engage in these behaviors several times a year. They assert their authority over the four corners of the region by releasing a witchcraft spell around it and set a crossroad over the top of it, so they can bind the region to their control. They are fervent in locking down the territory because they understand the power of having the region under their control. After learning this, my ministry has been fervent with physically going to the center of our city:

- Breaking these witchcraft spells.
- Binding the prince of the power of the air over our region.
- Commanding the demonic prince to remain eternally bound or to displace himself.
- Repenting and cleansing out the witchcraft spells released in the region.
- Releasing prayers that lock the region under the government of God.

I encourage you to implement this strategy. You will experience a significant authority and greater ease of contending for revival if you implement it.

➤ Witchcraft clogging and controlling the portals of the region. Sometimes witches and warlocks will use the portals of the saints to astral project into spiritual realms and transact witchcraft tasks in the spirit. Especially, if we have allowed things into our sphere that open the doors to sin and yield legal ground to the enemy. There are also instances where witches, warlocks, and demons will use your portal to track you. Whatever the case, I have found it beneficial to:

- Cleanse and fill the portal over my home, ministries, and region with the blood of Jesus and close off any entryways witches and demons are using to gain access to my portals.
- I decree that my portals are connected to the throne room of God, and release the blood of Jesus from my sphere to the throne of God. Demons and witches hate the purity of the blood, and they hate the judgment of God's throne. They will stop using your portals if the blood of Jesus is there to judge and torment them.
- I release blindness and judgment to witches and demons, and decree amnesia and a zapping to information they know about me.

Your portals are gateways. Be mindful of this and be mindful of what you entertain in your sphere. When you are a revivalist, the enemy is looking for anyway to snuff out your fire. Be mindful to repent quickly, cleanse, and close doors to engaging in anything that gives him and his imps access.

➢ Lack of God ordained or responsible watchmen at the regional gate.

➢ The season for things needing to die in the ground and atmosphere.

- Lack of cultivation and contending for an open heaven. The heavens have to be cultivated. Constant prayer, praise and worship, declaration of scriptures, declarations and prophetic words, promises, affirmations, and the exaltation of Jesus are necessary to maintain an open heaven. Depending on the mantle on your life and the region you live in, you may have to keep music, scriptures, and declarations playing in your home, ministry, and business to further assert continuous authority over your portals of heaven. This may sound like a bit much, but there are some idolatrous religions that offer up prayers and incense to their god 24 hours a day, and hire voodoo priests to keep the demonic altars burning for them and their families. The saints of God must grasp the power of consistency in lifting up Jesus where he effortlessly reigns in your sphere of influence.

- Strange fire versus pure praise and worship.

- Demonic spirits of religion, tradition, and legalism causing a blanket or wall of suffocation and death within the atmosphere of people, ministries, and the region. These strongholds snuff out and block the spirit of God from flowing freely. They love to linger in services and conferences to find a way to quench the Holy Spirit from operating. The heavens will be wide open, then something will go sideways, and there will be like a literal choking of the presence of God in the spirit realm. There are times where my team and I have experienced this choking physically when ministering. The spirit realm becomes dark and hard as the heaven's close, and we will begin to cough, and choke as these spirits wrap themselves around our necks. It is essential to recognize when the presence of God is waning, or the heavens are closing, and examine if it is God led or if you have been snuffed out by religion and tradition. As you are cultivating revival, it is important to take time to deal with these spirits when they operate. Break their grip, hammer down their walls, and exalt Jesus until the heavens reopen, and darkness is pushed back. Many ministries will recognize this is happening but do nothing. When you do nothing, the ground you just conquered in the spirit, is now being overtaken by demonic spirits. You must recognize you are in a battle for territory. You have the ultimate authority to reign and govern in that sphere. Demons and wickedness can only reign if you slack in claiming your rightful inheritance.

When you sense something is clogging the heavens and is resisting your authority, you can ask God to rend the heavens with his revival fire and blast down on the devil.

> *Isaiah 64:1-3 The Amplified Version - Oh, that You would rend the heavens and that You would come down, that the mountains might quake and flow down at Your presence — As when fire kindles the brushwood and the fire causes the waters to boil — to make Your name known to Your adversaries, that the nations may tremble at Your presence! When You did terrible things which we did not expect, You came down; the mountains quaked at Your presence.*

> *The Message Version - Oh, that you would rip open the heavens and descend, make the mountains shudder at your presence––As when a forest catches fire, as when fire makes a pot to boil––To shock your enemies into facing you, make the nations shake in their boots! You did terrible things we never expected, descended and made the mountains shudder at your presence.*

A rending is a violent tearing of the heavenlies. You have a right to ask God to tear the heavens, because Jesus already tore the veil, therefore, you have full access to the throne of God. Nothing should be separating you.

> *Matthew 27:50-51 Jesus, when he had cried again with a loud voice, yielded up the ghost. And, behold, the veil of the temple was rent in twain from the top to the bottom; and the earth did quake, and the rocks rent.*

> *Ephesians 3:9-12 And to make all men see what is the fellowship of the mystery, which from the beginning of the world hath been hid in God, who created all things by Jesus Christ: To the intent that now unto the principalities and powers in heavenly places might be known by the church the manifold wisdom of God, According to the eternal purpose which he purposed in Christ Jesus our Lord: In whom we have boldness and access with confidence by the faith of him.*

You can stand in this scripture and watch the Lord judge principalities on your behalf. But remember it requires bold faith as rending is a supernatural act and request for deliverance. God wants you to have access to his kingdom just as much as you want it for yourself. Trust him to honor you and to judge demonic powers on your behalf.

Chapter 14

Breaking Up Fallow Ground

This chapter is from my book entitled, "The Great Awakening; Igniting Regional Revival." It will be important to break up fallow grounds if you are going to govern and SHIFT atmospheres.

> *Psalm 63:1-5 O God, you are my God; earnestly I seek you; my soul thirsts for you; my flesh faints for you, as in a dry and weary land where there is no water. So I have looked upon you in the sanctuary, beholding your power and glory. Because your steadfast love is better than life, my lips will praise you. So I will bless you as long as I live; in your name I will lift up my hands. My soul will be satisfied as with fat and rich food, and my mouth will praise you with joyful lips.*

When we are cultivating and establishing the kingdom of God in the earth, we must contend from the ground just as we do the heavenlies. It is so important that we:

- ✓ Cleanse the land of past and present sin, famines and transgressions and break generational strongholds off the land (*Numbers, 14:18, Exodus 5:20, Jeremiah 2:6, Deuteronomy 28, Deuteronomy 32:10, Leviticus 26:38-42, Job 2:20, Ezekiel 20:5, Ezekiel 39, Haggai 1:10 Galatians 3:15*).

- ✓ Break up the hardness (*Hosea 10:12, Deuteronomy 8:23*).

- ✓ Cleanse waste and sickness from the land (*2Chronicles 7:14, Exodus 15:26, Micah 4:2, Matthew 4:15-16, Exodus 23:25, Revelations 22:2, 2Kings 2:19-21*).

Deuteronomy 28:21-23 The Lord shall send upon thee cursing, vexation, and rebuke, in all that thou settest thine hand unto for to do, until thou be destroyed, and until thou perish quickly; because of the wickedness of thy doings, whereby thou hast forsaken me. The Lord shall make the pestilence cleave unto thee, until he have consumed thee from off the land, whither thou goest to possess it. The Lord shall smite thee with a consumption, and with a fever, and with an inflammation, and with an extreme burning, and with the sword, and with blasting, and with mildew; and they shall pursue thee until thou perish. And thy heaven that is over thy head shall be brass, and the earth that is under thee shall be iron.

✓ Judge and displace demonic squatters and strongholds binding the land (*Ephesians 6:12, Luke 11:20, Matthew 12:28, Matthew 10:8, Matthew 18:18*).

✓ Judge demonic principalities and strongholds that may be lodged under the ground and under the waters (*Ephesians 6:10-12, Philippians 2:10, Matthew 10:8, Matthew 18:18*).

✓ Judge witches, warlocks, and demonic altars; Cleanse witchcraft and "destroy the high places. Do not be a "*good saint*" that shares the land with witchcraft as this grieves God. Do not allow them to remain in the land (*Exodus 22:18, Leviticus 20:6, Leviticus 6:27, Leviticus 26:30, Numbers 33:52, Jeremiah 7:31, 1Kings 3:2-3, 2Kings 15:3-4, 2Kings 23:8, Micah 5:10-12, 2Chronicles 34:3, Isaiah 8:19-22, Acts 19:17-20*).

✓ Claim Godly authority and jurisdiction over the land (*Genesis 1:27-28, Psalms 8:6, Hebrews 2:8*).

- ✓ Sow the kingdom and glory of God into the land (*Mark 1:15, Galatians 6:7-8, 2Corinthians 9:6, Matthew 13*).

- ✓ Reveal the unveiled glory instilled in the land.
    - *Isaiah 6:3 And one cried unto another, and said, Holy, holy, holy, is the LORD of hosts: the whole earth is full of his glory.*

    - *Numbers 14:21 But as truly as I live, all the earth shall be filled with the glory of the LORD.*

- ✓ Plow the womb of the land and region so it can be revived and fertile (*2Kings 2:18-22, Isaiah 54:1, Galatians 4:27, Psalms 127:5, Psalms 113:9*).

- ✓ Spiritually cultivate the land with the words, decrees, purposes, plans of the Lord, so it can begin to transform into Godly land (*Genesis 3:18, Exodus 32:25-26, Deuteronomy 11:14-15, Job 22:28, 2Chronicles 20:20, Isaiah 41:18, 1Corinthians 5:17*).

- ✓ Train and equip the people to be land and business owners (*Exodus 6:8, Deuteronomy 6:10, Deuteronomy 30:20-21, Matthew 5:5*).

- ✓ Train the people to establish the kingdom of God every place the soles of their feet tread (*Deuteronomy 1:4, Joshua 1:3*).

To implement the strategy above, we must first break up the iron and fallow ground.

> *Deuteronomy 28:23 And thy heaven that is over thy head shall be brass, and the earth that is under thee shall be iron.*

Iron means the ground is:

Harsh	Stronghold	Rigid	Ruthless
Oppressed	Cruel	Robust	Unbending
Shackled	Immovable	Stubborn	Unyielding

Hosea 10:12 Sow to yourselves in righteousness, reap in mercy; break up your fallow ground: for it is time to seek the LORD, till he come and rain righteousness upon you.

The Message Bible Sow righteousness, reap love. It's time to till (break up) the ready earth (the fallow Ground), it's time to dig in with God, Until he arrives with righteousness ripe for harvest.

Fallow means the ground is:

Untilled	Unplowable	Stale	Hard
Uncultivated	Depleted	Fruitless	Neglected
Unseeded	Dry	Infertile	Undeveloped
Inactive	Empty	Sterile	Unfarmed
Unattended	Spiritually Void	Parched	Vacant
Unplanted	Impoverished	Waste	Virgin
Slacked	Impotent	Asleep	Neglected

That is so sad. HELP US GOD!

Figure 1DryLand Picture from yessweeterthanhoney.wordpress.com

Though our regions appear to be plowed in the natural, spiritually, the ground of many of our regions are fallow.

The fact that much of our natural plowing lacks sufficient production to keep our regions healthy, successful, stable, and progressive is also proof of the spiritual fallow grounds in our regions. Seeming that most of our regions are consumed with demonic and worldly systems, laws, morals, and standards, this yields further revelation that the spiritual ground of our regions is fallow.

You know how some houses or buildings catch on fire, but after the fire, the structure of the house or building is still standing? We do not want that. We want everything to be consumed in the revival fire, so everything that is not of God is burned up and everything that is of him remains, is refined, transformed and is equipped for effective use beyond the fire. We want to break up the fallow ground in our lives, families, ministries, lands, and regions.

> *Hebrews 12:27-29 And this word, Yet once more, signifieth the removing of those things that are shaken, as of things that are made, that those things which cannot be shaken may remain. Wherefore we receiving a kingdom which cannot be moved, let us have grace, whereby we may serve God acceptably with reverence and godly fear: For our God is a consuming fire.*

To break up the fallow ground, we must cultivate a lifestyle of righteousness. As we are imputed to righteousness, we must become penetrable where the fire of God consumes us, becomes us, such that we are pliable and surrendered for God to work through us as a righteous seed infusing the earth.

As righteousness is used to break up the iron and fallow ground, it releases:

Rightness	Virtue	Justice	Righteous acts
Rectitude	Prosperity	Judgment	Righteous Government

Our righteousness has to be a literal seed of judgement fire and hammering when breaking up the ground.

116

Jeremiah 23:9 Does not my word burn like fire?" says the LORD. "Is it not like a mighty hammer that smashes a rock to pieces?

Holman Christian Standard Bible "Is not My word like fire"--this is the LORD's declaration--"and like a hammer that pulverizes rock?

<u>Dictionary.com defines *pulverize* as:</u>
1. to reduce to dust or powder, as by pounding or grinding
2. to demolish or crush completely
3. to defeat, hurt badly, render helpless

When God wreaks righteous judgment on the ground, he has no mercy.

Revelation 21:8 But the fearful, and unbelieving, and the abominable, and murderers, and whoremongers, and sorcerers, and idolaters, and all liars, shall have their part in the lake which burneth with fire and brimstone: which is the second death.

Genesis 19:24-25 Then the Lord rained upon Sodom and upon Gomorrah brimstone and fire from the Lord out of heaven; 25 And he overthrew those cities, and all the plain, and all the inhabitants of the cities, and that which grew upon the ground.

We must be like our Father when it comes to releasing righteous judgment on the land. We cannot have any mercy. **SHIFT!**

Chapter 15

Battering Prayers

Battering prayers break down fortified walls, gates, fortresses, and seizes. They allow you to break anything down that hinders you access to what God is saying is for you. Battering can be the use of repetitious words, scriptures, decrees, lyrics, sounds, movements, laws, standards, promises, or prophecies, to dismantle and crumble a blockage against you. You persistently pound and hammer, beating, blasting, damaging, wrecking, weakening and killing your target repeatedly until it yields way to you.

Britannica.com defines a *battering ram* as:

Battering ram, an ancient and medieval weapon consisting of a heavy timber, typically with a metal knob or point at the front. Such devices were used to batter down the gates or walls of a besieged city or castle. The ram itself, usually suspended by ropes from the roof of a movable shed, was swung back and forth by its operators against the besieged structure. The roof of the shed was usually covered with animal skins to protect the weapon's operators from bombardment with stones or fiery materials.

> *Micah 2:13 The breaker goes up before them; They break out, pass through the gate and go out by it. So their king goes on before them, And the LORD at their head."*

> *Ezekiel 4:2 Then lay siege against it, build a siege wall, raise up a ramp, pitch camps and place battering rams against it all around.*

> *Ezekiel 21:22 Into his right hand came the divination, 'Jerusalem,' to set battering rams, to open the mouth for*

slaughter, to lift up the voice with a battle cry, to set battering rams against the gates, to cast up ramps, to build a siege wall.

Ezekiel 26:9 *The blow of his battering rams he will direct against your walls, and with his axes he will break down your towers.*

Psalms 18:29 *For by thee I have run (blast) through a troop; and by my God have I leaped over a wall.*

2 Samuel 20:15 *They came and besieged him in Abel Beth-maacah, and they cast up a siege ramp against the city, and it stood by the rampart; and all the people who were with Joab were wreaking destruction in order to topple the wall.*

2 Kings 14:13 *Then Jehoash king of Israel captured Amaziah king of Judah, the son of Jehoash the son of Ahaziah, at Beth-shemesh, and came to Jerusalem and tore down the wall of Jerusalem from the Gate of Ephraim to the Corner Gate, 400 cubits.*

2 Chronicles 25:23 *Then Joash king of Israel captured Amaziah king of Judah, the son of Joash the son of Jehoahaz, at Beth-shemesh, and brought him to Jerusalem and tore down the wall of Jerusalem from the Gate of Ephraim to the Corner Gate, 400 cubits.*

Jeremiah 39:2 *in the eleventh year of Zedekiah, in the fourth month, in the ninth day of the month, the city wall was breached.*

2 Chronicles 36:19 *Then they burned the house of God and broke down the wall of Jerusalem, and burned all its fortified buildings with fire and destroyed all its valuable articles.*

Jeremiah 52:7 Then the city was broken into, and all the men of war fled and went forth from the city at night by way of the gate between the two walls which was by the king's garden, though the Chaldeans were all around the city. And they went by way of the Arabah.

Psalm 89:40 You have broken down all his walls; You have brought his strongholds to ruin.

Isaiah 24:12 Desolation is left in the city And the gate is battered to ruins.

Sometimes you will have to batter unforeseen walls, fortresses, obstructions, blockages, barriers, gates, and brass heavens, that have been erected in and around buildings, lands, atmospheres, communities, and regions. This battering can be done through continuous use of prayers, scriptures, promises, prophecies, songs, dance movements, and the weapons listed in Chapter 12. It will be important to know that your work is not in vain and the more you batter, the more you are breaking through the barrier that is hindering the atmosphere from SHIFTING from bondage to freedom.

Study the scriptures above to solidify the battering ram revelation inside your spirit. That way you will be quickened to use this prayer tactic during times when warring is difficult. You do not have to settle or give up. You can BATTER your way to breakthrough. **SHIFT!**

Chapter 16

Intercessory Watchman Prayers

Intercession means you are standing in the gap and warring on behalf of yourself, family members, loved ones, the body of Christ, people in general, generations and lineages, land, communities, regions, spheres, and nations. Intercession often times requires repentance on behalf of yourself, others, and what you are praying for. Repentance is not just words but a heart posture of sorrow for sins and a desire to change and be righteous for God. It is a posture to love what God loves and hate what he hates and a willingness to sacrifice sins, transgressions, and unpleasing pleasures for God's will, ways, and standards. You also intercede for miracles, signs, wonders, deliverance, healings, breakthrough, perseverance, endurance, advancement, and success.

> *1Timothy 2:1 I exhort therefore, that, first of all, supplications, prayers, intercessions, [and] giving of thanks, be made for all men.*

> *Matthew 18:19-20 Again I say unto you, That if two of you shall agree on earth as touching anything that they shall ask, it shall be done for them of my Father which is in heaven.*

> *Romans 8:26 Likewise the Spirit also helpeth our infirmities: for we know not what we should pray for as we ought: but the Spirit itself maketh intercession for us with groanings which cannot be uttered.*

> *Ephesians 6:18 Praying always with all prayer and supplication in the Spirit, and watching thereunto with all perseverance and supplication for all saints;*

John 15:7 If ye abide in me, and my words abide in you, ye shall ask what ye will, and it shall be done unto you.

John 16:23-24 And in that day ye shall ask me nothing. Verily, verily, I say unto you, Whatsoever ye shall ask the Father in my name, he will give [it] you.

Matthew 21:22 And all things, whatsoever ye shall ask in prayer, believing, ye shall receive.

An intercessory watchman has increased duties.

Isaiah 62:6-7 The Amplified Bible I have set watchmen upon your walls, O Jerusalem, who will never hold their peace day or night; you who [are His servants and by your prayers] put the Lord in remembrance [of His promises], keep not silence, And give Him no rest until He establishes Jerusalem and makes her a praise in the earth.

*Set is **paqad** in the Hebrew and means, "to be appointed officer, governor, judge, oversee, to avenge, charge, to be deposited."*

*Watchmen is **samar** in the Hebrew and means, "guard, protect, keeper, give heed."*

When using intercession to govern and SHIFT atmospheres you become the mediator for God to SHIFT heaven to earth. Intercession requires you to become a watchman on the wall in governing that atmosphere and consistently praying and contending for breakthrough until God establishes his will and purpose in that sphere. Your watchman position is not that of a normal intercession. You serve as an officer, a governor, a judge, an overseer, and an avenger for God.

- You establish laws, standards, and purposes of God.
- Determine what goes in and out of that atmosphere.
- Judge and avenge anything that defies the laws, standards, and purposes of God.
- You charge the atmosphere with God's word, will, and purposes so that it can be ripe for his will to come to pass.

The Message Bible I've posted watchmen on your walls, Jerusalem. Day and night they keep at it, praying, calling out, reminding God to remember. They are to give him no peace until he does what he said, until he makes Jerusalem famous as the City of Praise.

Chapter 17

Travailing Prayers

Some atmospheres will have to be birthed out. You will have to acquire the heart of God for the people, land, community, and region, and will have to labor over them like you would the birth of a child. I remember when my overseer visited and trained my team on the story of Hannah and shared this revelation with us. I did not comprehend it fully at that time. But as we continued to awaken revival reformation in our region, I understood everything she was imparting into us.

When you have a travailing heart for a region you love it like a child. You do not allow anyone to say or speak anything over the region, over your womb, into the vision or against the potential of your region. Like Hannah in *1Samuel 1* (study this chapter), you recognize the Penninahs that like to gloat and antagonize you about how great their region is, their vision is, and how well they are birthing and growing, while speaking death into who you are (*Verse 4*). They are constant reminders of what you do not have but long for. They are constant reminders of the potential of the fruit of your womb but not the reality of it. Like Hannah, you have a worthy portion of blessings, but the womb of your region is shut up (*Verse 5*). Yet, a constant desire to give birth, nurture, and see your region flourish is in you.

The Penninahs even become an adversary to you. They mock the atmospheres, regions, and visions you are striving to birth (*Verse 6*). Instead of being an understanding support, they become your rival. Their constant words of death and reminders of what you do not have causes vexation, affliction, anguish, distress, tribulation, and trouble to your soul. You will have to resist remaining bitter, resentful and contentious with them, and focus on offering up sacrifices of travail to the

Lord.

Others will not understand your travail, not even those that are close to you. They will want you to settle and will want you to be grateful for what you do have (*Verse 8*). But you will have to keep travailing and laboring for impregnation even when others believe you should give up. Even when others think it is not worth the agony you are experiencing. Even when people think you are crazy for wanting what you want as they do not know the desire that God has instilled in you.

Like Hannah, it will be important to take your heart for breakthrough to him, and remind him of the desire to give birth that he has placed in you (*Verse 10-12*). Let him heal the bitterness from your adversary and contend with him for favor and breakthrough for heaven on earth in your midst. Travailing will feel weird, look weird; you will appear one way to others but inwardly you will be praying and contending for what is rightfully yours (*Verse 12-16*). Even those who are spiritual may not recognize you are travailing. They will misunderstand what is happening to you which will be weird because you will expect them to have the eyes, ears, and vision of the Lord. But they will misspeak, misinterpret, and accuse you of being something you are not. You bring enlightenment to them in love and keep right on travailing. As your travail is not about their understanding, it is about what you know is in you to birth.

As you keep your eye on the prize, God will grant grace and open your womb to conceive (*Verse 17-20*). You will birth for the atmosphere, region, and vision and it will be a display and reminder that God heard and remembered you. Do not get caught up in gloating to those who taunted you, mocked you, did not support, understand, or believe in you. Instead focus on offering up what you have birthed back to God. Spend your energy nurturing and cultivating it in the glory and wellness of the Lord. Even as you nurture and help it to grow, make sure it relies on God and not you (*Verse 22-28*). Wean it from feeding from your bosom to feasting at the heart of Jesus. As then, it will become all he desires it to be and will fulfill the destiny to which is was birthed for.

Travailing prayers are a manifestation of the:
- Grieving heart of God.
- A grieving desire, purpose, or vision that God has placed in a person.
- Jesus making intercession for and through a person.
- Birthing forth of new things.
- Roaring and rending of God.
- Contending for breakthrough.

Travailing prayers are:
- Painfully, difficult or burdensome work.
- Requires toiling and exertion.
- Bitter, sore, vexing, distressing.
- Can cause pain, anguish or suffering resulting from mental or physical hardship.
- Can manifest wailing and uncontrollable crying and grieving.
- Can feel like the pain of childbirth.
- Have an adversary – a Penninah.
- Can be misunderstood, mocked, ridiculed, devalued, and contended against by onlookers.

Both men and women travail!

> *Jeremiah 30:5-6 For thus saith the Lord; We have heard a voice of trembling, of fear, and not of peace. Ask ye now, and see whether a man doth travail with child? wherefore do I see every man with his hands on his loins, as a woman in travail, and all faces are turned into paleness?*

Grief of the Heart of God

2Corinthians 7:10 *For godly sorrow worketh repentance to salvation not to be repented of: but the sorrow of the world worketh death.*

Psalms 126:5-6 *They that sow in tears shall reap in joy. He that goeth forth and weepeth, bearing precious seed, shall doubtless come again with rejoicing, bringing his sheaves with him.*

Ecclesiastes 3:4 *A time to weep, and a time to laugh; a time to mourn, and a time to dance.*

Daniel 7:15 *I Daniel was grieved in my spirit in the midst of my body, and the visions of my head troubled me."*

Daniel 8:27 *And I Daniel fainted, and was sick certain days; afterward I rose up, and did the king's business; and I was astonished at the vision, but none understood it.*

Daniel 10:8 *Therefore I was left alone, and saw this great vision, and there remained no strength in me: for my comeliness was turned in me into corruption, and I retained no strength.*

Jesus Intercession

Romans 8:26-27 *Likewise the Spirit also helpeth our infirmities: for we know not what we should pray for as we ought: but the Spirit itself maketh intercession for us with groanings which cannot be uttered. And he that searcheth the hearts knoweth what is the mind of the Spirit, because he maketh intercession for the saints according to the will of God.*

Verse 34 Who is he that condemneth? It is Christ that died, yea rather, that is risen again, who is even at the right hand of God, who also maketh intercession for us.

John 11:32-34 Then when Mary was come where Jesus was, and saw him, she fell down at his feet, saying unto him, Lord, if thou hadst been here, my brother had not died. When Jesus therefore saw her weeping, and the Jews also weeping which came with her, he groaned in the spirit, and was troubled, And said, Where have ye laid him? They said unto him, Lord, come and see. Jesus wept.

Verse 38 Jesus therefore again groaning in himself cometh to the grave. It was a cave, and a stone lay upon it. Jesus said, Take ye away the stone. Martha, the sister of him that was dead, saith unto him, Lord, by this time he stinketh: for he hath been dead four days. Jesus saith unto her, Said I not unto thee, that, if thou wouldest believe, thou shouldest see the glory of God?

Luke 22:41-44 And he was withdrawn from them about a stone's cast, and kneeled down, and prayed, Saying, Father, if thou be willing, remove this cup from me: nevertheless not my will, but thine, be done. And there appeared an angel unto him from heaven, strengthening him. And being in agony he prayed more earnestly: and his sweat was as it were great drops of blood falling down to the ground.

Isaiah 53:11-12 He shall see of the travail of his soul, and shall be satisfied: by his knowledge shall my righteous servant justify many; for he shall bear their iniquities. Therefore will I divide him a portion with the great, and he shall divide the spoil with the strong; because he hath poured out his soul unto death: and he was numbered with the transgressors; and he bare the sin of many, and made intercession for the transgressors.

Birthing

John 3:6 That which is born of the flesh is flesh, and that which is born of the Spirit is spirit"

Galatians 4:19 My little children, of whom I travail in birth again until Christ be formed in you.

Isaiah 66:8-11 Who hath heard such a thing? who hath seen such things? Shall the earth be made to bring forth in one day? or shall a nation be born at once? for as soon as Zion travailed, she brought forth her children.

Shall I bring to the birth, and not cause to bring forth? saith the Lord: shall I cause to bring forth, and shut the womb? saith thy God.

Rejoice ye with Jerusalem, and be glad with her, all ye that love her: rejoice for joy with her, all ye that mourn for her: That ye may suck, and be satisfied with the breasts of her consolations; that ye may milk out, and be delighted with the abundance of her glory.

Isaiah 43:19 Behold, I will do a new thing, Now it shall spring (birth) forth; Shall you not know it?

Roaring & Rending

*Isaiah 42:13 The LORD shall go forth as a mighty man, he shall stir up jealousy like a man of war: he shall cry, yea, roar; he shall prevail against his enemies. (**The Lord roars**).*

Jeremiah 25:30 Therefore prophesy thou against them all these words, and say unto them, The LORD shall roar from on high, and utter his voice from his holy habitation; he shall mightily roar upon his habitation; he shall give a shout, as they that tread the grapes, against all the inhabitants of the earth.

Isaiah 51:15 *For I am the Lord your God who stirs up the sea so that its waves roar - His name is Yahweh of Hosts.*

Acts 2:2 *International Standard Bible Suddenly, a sound like the roar of a mighty windstorm came from heaven and filled the whole house where they were sitting.* ***(The Holy Ghost roars).***

Psalm 104:21 *The young lions roar after their prey, and seek their meat from God.* ***(We can roar as we war against the enemy).***

Isaiah 5:29 *Their roaring shall be like a lion, they shall roar like young lions: yea, they shall* ***roar****, and lay hold of the prey, and shall carry it away safe, and none shall deliver it.*

Isaiah 13:4 *A sound, a noise is on the mountains, the likeness of many people! A sound of the roar of [the] kingdoms, of nations gathering! Yahweh of hosts is mustering an army for battle.*

Isaiah 17:12 *Ah! The roar of many peoples- they roar like the roaring of the seas. The raging of the nations- they rage like the raging of mighty waters.*

Psalms 42:7 *Deep calls to deep in the roar of Your waterfalls; all Your breakers and Your billows have swept over me.* ***(Those deep in God and in prayer can roar one to another; there can be a travail from God to us and vice versa).***

Psalm 46:6 *Nations roar, kingdoms shake; he utters his voice, the earth melts.* **(God causes a roaring in nations; nations can also travail unto God).**

Hosea 11:10 *They shall walk after the LORD: he shall roar like a lion: when he shall roar, then the children shall tremble from the west.*

Hosea 13:8 *I will encounter them like a bear robbed of her cubs, And I will tear open their chests; There I will also devour them like a lioness, As a wild beast would tear them.*

Jeremiah 25:38 *He has left His hiding place like the lion; For their land has become a horror Because of the fierceness of the oppressing sword And because of His fierce anger."*

Breakthrough

Genesis 32:24-26 *Jacob was left alone, and a man wrestled with him until daybreak. And when he saw that he had not prevailed against him, he touched the socket of his thigh; so the socket of Jacob's thigh was dislocated while he wrestled with him. Then he said, 'Let me go, for the dawn is breaking.' But he said, 'I will not let you go unless you bless me.'"*

Ephesians 6:11-12 The Amplified Bible *Put on God's whole armor [the armor of a heavy-armed soldier, which God supplies], that you may be able successfully to stand up against all the strategies and the deceits of the devil. For we are not wrestling with flesh and blood [contending only with physical opponents], but against the despotisms, against [the master spirits who are] the world rulers of this present darkness, against the spirit forces of wickedness in the heavenly (supernatural) sphere."*

John 16:21 *A woman, when she is in labor, has sorrow because her hour has come; but as soon as she has given birth*

131

to the child, she no longer remembers the anguish, for joy that a human being has been born into the world.

Chapter 18

Prophecy & Prayer

Prophecy is the Greek word **propheteia**, which is the amalgamation of two other words, **pro**, meaning *forth* and **phemi**, meaning *to speak*.

Prophesying means you are edifying, comforting, and exhorting people (*1Corinthians 14:3*) in the promises, will, purposes, and intents of the Lord, foretelling future events, revealing the truths, identity, abilities, and capabilities of Jesus (the testimony of Jesus is the spirit of prophecy *Revelation 19:10*).

> *1Corinthians 14:3 But he that prophesieth speaketh unto men to edification, and exhortation, and comfort.*

> *Revelation 19:10 And I fell at his feet to worship him. And he said unto me, See thou do it not: I am thy fellow servant, and of thy brethren that have the testimony of Jesus: worship God: for the testimony of Jesus is the spirit of prophecy.*

A prophet is a person who:
- Teaches, interprets, or proclaims the will of God.
- Foretells events or future endeavors.
- Advocates and speaks innovatively for a cause or purpose.

If a person is in the office of a prophet, they can judge, rebuke, correct, direct, display the anger of the Lord to a people, region, or nation.

Prophecies are excellent weapons against the enemy because once God speaks a matter it cannot return unto him void.

> *Isiah 55:11 So shall my word be that goeth forth out of my mouth: it shall not return unto me void, but it shall*

accomplish that which I please, and it shall prosper in the thing whereto I sent it.

In this scripture *"word"* means *"commandment, power, vision, purpose. So prophecies are destined to prosper and have an expected end of purpose."*

> *Jeremiah 29:11 For I know the thoughts that I think toward you, saith the LORD, thoughts of peace, and not of evil, to give you an expected end.*

<u>Thoughts</u> is the Hebrew word ***machashebeth*** <u>meaning</u>:
1. a contrivance, machine, or (abstractly) intention
2. plan (whether bad, a plot; or good, advice): — cunning (work)
3. curious work, device(-sed), imagination, invented, means, purpose

God's thoughts work like a machine or invention to produce what he has purposed for you.

It is important to note that the word will not return unto GOD void. Your governing of the word determines whether it returns unto YOU void or if it produces in your life.

When you are birthing destiny, visions, and atmospheres, God will give you prophetic promises and visions regarding his intents and desires. You will have to work the strategies of the prophecies but also stand believing while continuing to pray them out loud into the atmosphere to see them come to pass; and so you can receive further insight and strategy of how to bring them to pass. Prophecy is like a seed. It blossoms to a full invention as you align with it and grow into it. You know the future of what is to come and you continue to walk in and to that word as it comes to pass on your behalf.

Praying your prophecies are part of bringing them to pass. It is as if you become an intercessory watchman and Hannah of travail over what God has spoken. You pray them like decrees to consistently establish them in the airways and frequencies and watch them flourish in your midst. It is ok to remind God regarding what he has spoken. He enjoys when we have a passion and travail to see his prophecies manifest in our lives. We are more likely to govern them properly and maintain a healthy heart and character that produces sustaining success.

Chapter 19

Soaking Prayers

Soaking prayers are utilized:

- During a time of resting from warfare.

  o *Jeremiah 31:5 New Living Bible I will refresh the weary and satisfy the faint.*

  o *Ecclesiastes 3:8 A time to love and a time to hate, a time for war and a time for peace.*

- During a time of rest in the middle of warfare.

  o *Exodus 14:14 The Lord will fight for you while you [only need to] keep silent and remain calm.*

- During a time of resting from ministry.

  o *Mark 6:31 And he said to them, "Come away by yourselves to a desolate place and rest a while." For many were coming and going, and they had no leisure even to eat.*

  o *Matthew 11:28 Come to Me, all who are weary and heavily burdened [by religious rituals that provide no peace], and I will give you rest [refreshing your souls with salvation].*

- When needing refreshing, renewal or peace.

  o *Proverbs 11:25 New Living Bible A generous person will prosper; whoever refreshes others will be refreshed.*

  o *Isaiah 40:31 But those who hope in the LORD will renew their strength. They will soar on wings like eagles; they will run and not grow weary, they will walk and not be faint.*

- *Isaiah 26:3 Thou wilt keep [him] in perfect peace, [whose] mind [is] stayed [on thee]: because he trusteth in thee.*

- During a time of expectation.

  - *Psalms 5:3 In the morning, Lord, you hear my voice; in the morning I lay my requests before you and wait expectantly.*

  - *Psalms 130:5 I wait for the Lord, my whole being waits, and in his word I put my hope.*

- During times of cleansing of sin issues, deliverance and healing.

  - *Acts 3:19 Repent, then, and turn to God, so that your sins may be wiped out, that times of refreshing may come from the Lord.*

  - *Psalms 130:15 For thus said the Lord God, the Holy One of Israel, "In returning and rest you shall be saved; in quietness and in trust shall be your strength.*

- When needing answers and guidance from the Lord.

  - *Psalms 40:1 I waited patiently for the Lord; he turned to me and heard my cry.*

- When wanting to be consumed by a characteristic or fruit of God. For example, sometimes I soak myself in the glory of God, the power of God, and the boldness of God. I may lay down in his presence or I may be up moving about and I may meditate or declare out loud that I am being soaked in that characteristic or fruit (i.e. I soak myself in the glory of God. I consume myself in the glory of God. I am being drenched in the glory of God).

- *John 15:4* Abide in me, and I in you. As the branch cannot bear fruit of itself, except it abide in the vine; no more can ye, except ye abide in me.

- *Philippians 4:8* Finally, brethren, whatsoever things are true, whatsoever things [are] honest, whatsoever things [are] just, whatsoever things [are] pure, whatsoever things [are] lovely, whatsoever things [are] of good report; if [there be] any virtue, and if [there be] any praise, think on these things.

- Meditating on God's word and solidifying the scriptures, promises, or prophecies in one's spirit.

  - *Joshua 1:8* This book of the law shall not depart out of thy mouth; but thou shalt meditate therein day and night, that thou mayest observe to do according to all that is written therein: for then thou shalt make thy way prosperous, and then thou shalt have good success.

  - *Psalms 19:14* Let the words of my mouth, and the meditation of my heart, be acceptable in thy sight, O LORD, my strength, and my redeemer.

  - *Psalms 49:3* My mouth shall speak of wisdom; and the meditation of my heart [shall be] of understanding.

  - *Psalms 119:11* Thy word have I hid in mine heart, that I might not sin against thee.

  - *Psalms 119:15* I will meditate in thy precepts, and have respect unto thy ways.

  - *Psalms 119:97-99* O how love I thy law! it is my meditation all the day. Thou through thy commandments hast made me wiser than mine enemies: for they are ever with me. I have more understanding than all my teachers: for thy testimonies are my meditation.

- *Proverbs 4:20-22 My son, attend to my words; incline thine ear unto my sayings. Let them not depart from thine eyes; keep them in the midst of thine heart. For they are life unto those that find them, and health to all their flesh.*

- When needing refreshing sleep. When needing to release the day to God before going to sleep.

  - *Psalms 63:6 When I remember You on my bed, I meditate on You in the night watches.*

  - *Psalms 104:34 My meditation of him shall be sweet: I will be glad in the LORD.*

When soaking, the focus is on:
  - Communing with God.
  - Building greater covenant and relationship with God.
  - Becoming like God – God identity.
  - Becoming consumed with the fruit, characteristics, word, and presence of God.
  - Relying on God, trusting God, building faith in God.
  - Releasing life issues and challenges to God.
  - Waiting on God for further guidance, breakthrough, or to handle a matter for you.
  - Being delivered, healed, and transformed by God.

- I believe soaking is the greatest way to be endued with power. We need power to assert authority over demons and spheres.

  Luke 24:49 *And, behold, I send the promise of my Father upon you: but tarry ye in the city of Jerusalem, until ye be endued with power from on high.*

  <u>Power</u> is ***dynamis*** or ***dunamis*** <u>in the Greek and means:</u>

1. force (literally or figuratively); specially, miraculous power (usually by implication, a miracle itself)
2. ability, abundance, might, worker of miracles
3. strength, violence, mighty (wonderful) work, ability, inherent power
4. power residing in a thing by virtue of its nature, or which a person or thing exerts and puts forth
5. power for performing miracles, moral power and excellence of soul, the power and influence which belong to riches and wealth, power consisting in or resting upon armies, forces, hosts

Enduing denotes a sinking into a garment such as a piece of clothing, a mantle, or a vestment. The power of God literally becomes a mantle upon your mantle. It is like an activation mantle as it SHIFTS your mantle into operating from a greater dimension of power and authority. We are endued when we receive the infilling of the Holy Spirit but we can receive times of endowment and even fresh baptisms of the Holy Spirit when we spend time communing, waiting, and resting in the presence of the Lord. We can soak ourselves in his power and be infused by his might, virtue, strength, and miracle working presence.

- In addition to soaking yourself in God, you can soak an atmosphere, home, building, land, ministry, business, community, and region in God.

  o *2Chronicles 7:15-16 Now my eyes will be open and my ears attentive to the prayer that is made in this place. For now I have chosen and consecrated this house that my name may be there forever. My eyes and my heart will be there for all time.* **(Consecration is a set aside time of sanctification, purification, cleansing, and absorbing the presence of the Lord).**

- *Isaiah 44:3,4 For I will pour water upon him that is thirsty, and floods upon the dry ground: I will pour my spirit upon thy seed, and my blessing upon thine offspring.*

- *Isaiah 32:15 Until the spirit be poured upon us from on high, and the wilderness be a fruitful field, and the fruitful field be counted for a forest.*

- You can also ask for an unveiling and revealing of the glory that is already here in the earth.

  - *Psalms 72:19 Praise be to his glorious name forever; may the whole earth be filled with his glory. Amen and Amen.*

  - *Isaiah 6:3 And one cried unto another, and said, Holy, holy, holy, is the LORD of hosts: the whole earth is full of his glory.*

  - *Numbers 14:21 Yet as surely as I live and as surely as the whole earth is filled with the glory of the LORD.*

  - *Isaiah 40:5 And the glory of the LORD will be revealed, and all mankind together will see it. For the mouth of the LORD has spoken.*

You can soak to music or without. You can set a specific time aside for soaking and consecration or you can take moments to soak throughout the day or soak while you are doing other tasks. Though I have a specific daily prayer time, I commune with God all throughout the day. I also take moments to soak myself in whatever I may need at the time. I can be in my car, writing a report, washing dishes, walking down the street. And I will begin to focus on God and soaking myself in his love, joy, peace, power, glory, truth, grace, laughter, patience, strength, rejuvenation, and goodness. I may do this out loud or within myself. I may meditate on a scripture and command it to become the consumption of me. I may begin to soak my surroundings in the goodness, glory, and blessings of God. I may begin to command heaven to come to earth and declare that my region is being consumed and absorbed in the atmosphere of heaven. I may ask for a revealing of the glory that is already in the earth and for it to become more tangible, weightier, and renewing to myself and the region. I am not warring at this time, I am in a posture of receiving and trusting that even if I do not feel anything God is granting my request. Often times, I begin to have manifestations of whatever portion of God I am soaking myself in.

Soaking prayer is essential when having a mandate of governing and SHIFTING atmospheres. This mandate can be hard work and require intense times and seasons of plowing, cultivating, warring, interceding, and travailing for a sustaining establishing of the kingdom of heaven in your midst. It will be important to take moments, times, and seasons to soak and refresh or soak to become fueled with more of God. Ministries and teams should even spend time soaking and refueling together. Soaking prayer nights are always in order. You can also use this time to soak the atmosphere of your ministry, land, and building. God wants to commune with you, abide in and around you, and inhabit all that concerns you. Allow his full identity to reign in you by making it your life's mission to be full of him. **SHIFT!**

Chapter 20

Team Keys

Understanding Realms, Power, and Order

Prayer Boldness

When you pray with a team, seek to pray from the same realm of authority and power and to go higher than the person who prayed before you. Be cognizant of not SHIFTING to a lower realm by not praying boldly, not praying intensely, or being in a different realm than them. This can happen by being in a realm of worship when they are in a realm of war or being in a realm of war when they are in a realm of bold faith or declaration. Another example of this is when you pray through a realm of fear, comparison or competition rather than knowing we are a team and your mantle and prayer style is just as important as everyone else's. Or, when it is your turn you pray outside of the realm we are in because you never taped in due to not really being engaged in the prayer.

It is important to open your mouth and pray with boldness and from your loins.

> *Jeremiah 1:17-19 Lexham English Bible But you, you must gird your loins, and stand, and speak to them all that I command you. Do not be afraid of them, or I will shatter you before them. Now look, I have made you today as a fortified city and as an iron pillar and a bronze wall against all the land, against the kings of Judah, against its princes, against its priests, and against the people of the land. And they will fight against you but they will not prevail against you, for I am with you," declares Yahweh, "to deliver you."*

Ephesians 6:14 Stand therefore, having your loins girt about with truth, and having on the breastplate of righteousness.

Loins are the place where the Hebrews believe our generative power (semen) resided - procreative power.

Mumbling prayers does not move devils. Mumbling prayer actually exposes your insecurities, condemnations, shames, jealousies, and fears. Mumbling prayers produce a false or unhealthy reality, and an emotional, earthly, or demonic atmosphere. The devil uses these ungodly attributes to assert authority over you and to hinder your prayers. You do not have to yell but you do need to pray from your loins - your stomach - where the fullness of the Holy Spirit can be charged, proactive, procreative, and where the fullness of your authority can be released. As the Holy Spirit is activated, he overrides your unhealthy or human perceptions and postures you inside your God reality, where the atmosphere becomes the truth of who you are in God and who he is in you.

Prayer Team Unity

Often when we know someone is praying something that is not of God or is not praying with authority, we are dreading it while mumbling and grumbling inside ourselves, or looking around for someone to agree with how sucky that person is. As a teammate, you should be holding that person's hands and helping to SHIFT them into the victory WE need, for when they suck, we all suck and go down with them. You do not watch them sink, you gird them up by interceding for them and SHIFTING them to where they are covered by you and the team as they complete their part of the prayer mission. Then later you encourage them, while also providing some constructive feedback and keys so they can grow in their prayer authority.

> *Exodus 17:12-14 But Moses' hands were heavy; and they took a stone, and put it under him, and he sat thereon; and Aaron and Hur stayed up his hands, the one on the one side, and the other on the other side; and his hands were steady until the going down of the sun. And Joshua discomfited Amalek and his people with the edge of the sword. And the Lord said unto Moses, Write this for a memorial in a book, and rehearse it in the ears of Joshua: for I will utterly put out the remembrance of Amalek from under heaven.*

<u>*Heavy* in this scripture means:</u>
1. in a bad sense (severe, difficult, stupid)
2. (so) negatively great, grievous, hard(-ened), (too) heavy(-ier)
3. laden, much, slow, sore, thick

Moses' hands were grievous, weak, weary, and hurting. His teammates postured him in a place of safety and comfort and then supported him in his part of the mission until the battle was won. If someone is praying in a lower realm and you know they are new to praying, insecure, fearful, weary, afflicted, bound, grievous, burdened, or being attacked, do not succumb to their realm. Use your prayers to posture them in a place of protection and relief. Then continue to pray from the realm you know God is in and intercede for them to be snatched up into that realm. Praying from a lower realm allows the enemy to bind and imprison them, you, the team and the atmosphere, and gives room for him to regain territory in the spirit and natural realm of your lives and whatever it is you all are praying for. You can carry the person that is praying by maintaining the realm of authority that God has you in. As they are held up, the team is held up and unity in and of itself breaks you all through to the victory. **SHIFT!**

Unity Of Praying In Tongues

It is important to know that your prayer language is a full real language.

> *Acts 2:1-11 When the day of Pentecost had come, they were all together in one place. And suddenly there came from heaven a noise like a violent rushing wind, and it filled the whole house where they were sitting. And there appeared to them tongues as of fire distributing themselves, and they rested on each one of them. read more.*
>
> *And they were all filled with the Holy Spirit and began to speak with other tongues, as the Spirit was giving them utterance. Now there were Jews living in Jerusalem, devout men from every nation under heaven. And when this sound occurred, the crowd came together, and were bewildered because each one of them was hearing them speak in his own language. They were amazed and astonished, saying, "Why, are not all these who are speaking Galileans? "And how is it that we each hear them in our own language to which we were born? "Parthians and Medes and Elamites, and residents of Mesopotamia, Judea and Cappadocia, Pontus and Asia, Phrygia and Pamphylia, Egypt and the districts of Libya around Cyrene, and visitors from Rome, both Jews and proselytes, Cretans and Arabs--we hear them in our own tongues speaking of the mighty deeds of God."*

Utterance is **apophtheggomai** in the Greek and means:
1. to enunciate plainly, i.e. declare: — say, speak forth, utterance.
2. to speak out, speak forth, pronounce

146

3. not a word of everyday speech but one "belonging to dignified and elevated discourse"

Your precise language comes forth as you open your mouth and truly make a conscious effort to articulate what the Holy Spirit is speaking through you. This also should be bellowed from your loins - your stomach - and you should not mumble or speak softly but be declarative in your speech and speaking forth the oracles of God. This is a dignified and elevated discourse that defies earthly potential, possibility, and demonic hindrances. Speaking in our prayer language is a supernatural phenomenon that totally puts God in charge and produces the miracles, signs, and wonders of heaven. People can misunderstand it, but no one can deny the power and unity it displays, even with us speaking different languages.

Teams should spend time praying in their Holy Spirit tongues together and have times of praying in tongues together to govern and SHIFT atmospheres. On the day of Pentecost, they were all waiting in unity on the Holy Spirit and when he filled them and the room, it SHIFTED in the supernatural language, power, presence, and kingdom of God. They got caught up in the experience itself and trying to explain it to onlookers but we can only imagine the miracles, signs, wonders, prophecy, etc. that could have manifested at that moment if they would have remained totally engulfed in what God was doing. With a Holy Spirit tongue talking team, you can have these Pentecost moments as much as you want and watch Joel's prophecy be continually fulfilled in your midst.

> *Acts 2: 15 -20 For these are not drunken, as ye suppose, seeing it is but the third hour of the day. But this is that which was spoken by the prophet Joel; And it shall come to pass in the last days, saith God, I will pour out of my Spirit upon all flesh: and your sons and your daughters shall prophesy, and your young men shall see visions, and your*

old men shall dream dreams: And on my servants and on my handmaidens I will pour out in those days of my Spirit; and they shall prophesy: And I will shew wonders in heaven above, and signs in the earth beneath; blood, and fire, and vapour of smoke: The sun shall be turned into darkness, and the moon into blood, before the great and notable day of the Lord come.

Team Discernment Of Heavenly Realms

When praying, especially if you are leading the prayer assignment or chosen to pray, seek to discern where the team is in heavenly realms, and where God wants to take the team.

1. The natural/physical realm – the earth realm - is the 1st heaven. It generally is self-focused, issue focused, emotional, carnal, material minded, and worldly. We should never pray from this place. *1John 2:16 New Living Bible For the world offers only a craving for physical pleasure, a craving for everything we see, and pride in our achievements and possessions. These are not from the Father, but are from this world.*

2. The sky that we can see along with the galaxies, spheres, and REALMS that we cannot see with the natural eye, is the 2nd heaven. The 2nd heaven is where principalities and powers, witches and warlock, wicked and ignorant people who desire power and fame operate. This 2nd heaven tends to be depressed, oppressive, sullen, dark, gloomy, double minded, uncertain, indefinite, shady, unclear, blurred in spiritual vision and sight, fuzzy, lukewarm, idolatrous, demonic, stronghold, prone to witchcraft, mixed with witchcraft and godly or spiritual truths; concealed with false truths and hidden motives. We are to govern over these

148

realms but not pray and live in these realms.
Ephesians 6:12 New Living Bible *For we are not fighting against flesh-and-blood enemies, but against evil rulers and authorities of the unseen world, against mighty powers in this dark world, and against evil spirits in the heavenly places.*

3. The kingdom of God is the 3rd heaven. The 3rd heaven has all authority over the first and the second heaven. The 3rd heaven is pure, holy, righteous, virtuous, just, God focused, producing of God's report, ground in godly truth and standards, liberated, accelerated, has the potential for acceleration and upward mobility, potent, creative, fruitful, miraculous, delivering, healing, empowering, supportive, all powerful, demonstrative, judgmental and resistant to the demonic, carnal, haughty, and worldly. The 3rd heaven has levels and dimensions we can tap into. This is an infinite realm so we can always go higher and deeper in maturity and dimensional SHIFT inside the 3rd heaven. The more we govern and operate inside the 3rd heaven, the more the spheres of these realms are unveiled to us. We should always pray from the 3rd heaven realms. ***Matthew 6:9-13*** *After this manner therefore pray ye: Our Father which art in heaven, Hallowed be thy name. Thy kingdom come, Thy will be done in earth, as it is in heaven. Give us this day our daily bread. And forgive us our debts, as we forgive our debtors. And lead us not into temptation, but deliver us from evil: For thine is the kingdom, and the power, and the glory, for ever. Amen.*

Learning the three heavenly spheres and their characteristics, helps you to discern when you are not in a 3rd heaven realm and when you need to SHIFT deeper and higher inside of this sphere. When praying, it is important to make sure you SHIFT the team to a place where by the time you all finish praying, a release of breakthrough is tangible and evident. This means you are to be intentional in praying for breakthrough and never praying just to say you prayed. You should always seek to SHIFT out of the 1st and 2nd heaven quickly, but also to live in the 3rd heavens, encounter God, encounter levels and dimensions of heaven, gain the vision and knowledge of heaven, know what God desires in that prayer time, and bring heaven to earth.

Practice daily discerning what heavenly sphere you are in and being mindful to live and reign from the 3rd heavens. This will make your discernment keener as you pray with your team or seek to SHIFT an atmosphere in a public setting.

First Man Up

When you are first to pray, you want to establish the team in heavenly realms. You do this by exalting Jesus' Lordship over everything, commanding the kingdom to come to earth, calling forth angelic help, hedging the team inside his governmental rule, establishing bloodlines and fires walls in and around the team, contending against any principalities and powers, witches and warlocks, sins, transgressions that try to reign with him, and declaring his kingdom, power, and glory in our midst.

> *Mathew 6:9-13 After this manner therefore pray ye: Our Father which art in heaven, Hallowed be thy name. Thy kingdom come, Thy will be done in earth, as it is in heaven. Give us this day our daily bread. And forgive us our debts, as we forgive our debtors. And lead us not into temptation, but deliver us from evil: For thine is the kingdom, and the power, and the glory, for ever. Amen.*

Psalms 100:4 Enter into his gates (heavenlies) with thanksgiving, and into his courts (throne room) with praise (exaltation): be thankful (adoration) unto him, and bless his name.

Protocol & Order

You always want to stay in alignment with your assignment that is given and what is being prayed. Only interject other assignments if they line up with what is already being prayed. Do not use the prayer time as an opportunity to interject your own motives or plans as this manipulates the team and God, and SHIFTS the prayers to a 1st heaven posture.

It is not your job to rebuke the team or the people unless you are a leader of the prayer team or over that assignment. If you feel God is leading you to rebuke, pray your assignment then let the leader know what you are sensing. They will decide if you should release it or if they should release it, or if it is something that should be released and prayed for at a later time. This is important because doing things out of order can quench the Holy Spirit and SHIFT the prayer to a place God is not saying at that time, while also giving entry to the devil.

Do not break rank. Pray when it is your turn and do not interject yourself as others are praying or pray over the top of them. If you sense something should be further prayed in that area, let the leader know and they will give further directions in that area.

We have an established ending on our KSM prayer team where the person before the next person who is to pray will end their prayer by saying *"In Jesus Name"* and will keep speaking in tongues to hold our rank and position in the spirit realm until the next person starts praying. I suggest this for other teams as well. It helps to flow in unity, from one prayer assignment to another, while maintaining a spiritual flow. It is important to know when it is your turn to pray so you can immediately take position. Team prayer operates like an army. There is no laxing on the battleground. Laxing causes infiltration and catastrophes. We are intentional in supporting and covering others while they are praying and quickly getting into position so we can further advance to victory. Be sensitive to the atmosphere, the Holy Spirit, and what God is doing. Do not use this time as an opportunity to talk or share, especially when it does not relate to what has been prayed and what God is doing in the atmosphere. Idle chatter, impure motives for sharing, foolish banter, carnal comments or unnecessary conversations, can quench the Holy Spirit and lend ground back to the enemy that was just snatched from hell. When asked if you have anything to share, make sure it is in alignment with what God is doing at that time or in alignment with what is being discussed, explored, and prayed at that time. If it is not, submit it to the leader or an elder in a text message, via phone, or in person so it can be presented at the appropriate time.

Scriptural Reinforcement

During team prayer, seek to implement as much biblical word into your prayer as possible. Be consistent in studying the word so you can utilize scripture to solidify and enforce authority regarding what you are praying. If you get a prayer assignment, ask God to give you scriptures on the subject, or focus on studying scriptures that speak forth God's promises and purposes in that area; and that demonstrate God's authority and your authority and right as a kingdom heir to have what you are praying for.

Chapter 21

The Power of Distractions

By: Minister Reenita Keys
Leader & Prophet of Kingdom Shifters Ministries Prayer Team

The ministry of prayer is considered an art for many intercessors. It is the strongest form of communication no matter the level of prayer you have been exposed to. With any line of communication, our surroundings may interrupt the strength of the connection. Distractions are used to paralyze the SHIFTS, transitions, breakthroughs, and so much more. Distractions work against us to dismantle our focus, submission, posture, and alignment needed to carry out an assignment. Distractions cause intercessors to focus on frivolous oppositions that disconnect them from being God-focused. If you are not careful, distractions can cause you to abort assignments and missions at hand. I want to identify a few distractions and how these subtle mind-binding tactics contend against intercessors, ministries, and corporate prayer teams.

Firstly, I want to define the word distraction to lay down a clear foundation.

Merriam-Webster defines *distractions* as:

> 1. Something that distracts: an object that directs one's attention away from something
>
> 2. The act of distracting or the state of being distracted

From a spiritual standpoint, distractions are missiles of destruction used to dismantle your ability to connect to God, your team, and personal development. Distractions will unknowingly cause the flesh to override what you deem "important" in that moment. Anything beneath this threshold, will unconsciously align your actions to this invisible list of importance. You must press and kill the tactics of the flesh daily. If you allow your flesh to have the authority over your spirit man, you will find yourself in an idle place.

> **Romans 8:13** says, *"For if you live according to the flesh you will die, but if by the Spirit you put to death the deeds of the body, you will live"* (**English Standard Version**).

As you can see, if you do not take authority over the power of distractions you are living by the laws of the flesh. Operating from this realm can cause your growth, development, foundation, and legacy to die. It is easy to take on false spiritual WebMD ailments and symptoms that plan your demise. From this stance, we become our own physician placing labels upon our head. Our misdiagnoses for being easily distracted is merely a blanket for the excuses we make. You have been groomed by society to believe it is okay to have the attention span of a goldfish. The devil is a liar! If you cannot stay focused for more than 3 seconds, where is your heart postured? We make time for the things we want to sow our time into. This principle applies to our ability to stay focused on the tasks and goals. Have you ever noticed it is easy for you to binge on a television series for hours? I find it thought provoking that many cannot focus in a time of prayer but effortlessly gorge themselves with defilement each day. The powers of darkness work in the subtlest of ways. If we are not attentive to the enemy's tactics, we will continue to live a step behind where God wants us to be.

Distractions come to paralyze prayer ministries. If your team members are not marching in a synchronized state, the enemy can slide through the cracks causing an ambush. The devil knows that he cannot control the power of God. However, he will do all he can to cause spiritual delays. Killing the flesh is not just something you do when you are a babe in Christ. It is a continuous journey where we become martyrs for God. Effective fervent prayers can only take place if you are willing to allow your knees to speak louder than your shoulders. This is a reason we see many in the body of Christ falling to the devices of the enemy. Do not allow comparison, pride, shallowness, self-exaltation, or religious clichés to steal the true focus for prayer and intercession. We cannot allow distractions to guide us into having a falsified heart for intercession. We must rise up as intercessors bearing the marks of being a living sacrifice.

CORPORATE PRAYER GATHERINGS

Distractions can hit a prayer team in the most cunning ways. Often times, team members become distracted in prayer gatherings by the elements of their environment, posture, and connectivity. When intercessors become familiar with their surroundings, it is easy to fall into desensitization. To dismantle the power of distractions, we must pinpoint and expose these subtle doors that work to discombobulate teams, ministries, and churches. We have compiled a list of ways intercessors become distracted by their environments on prayer calls.

1. **Having a Spontaneous Unction to Plan Your Day**.

   Intercessors become distracted by planning out their day while on a prayer call or prayer meeting. This is the most common way the enemy invades corporate prayer. Your focus is not fully submitted to the assignment at hand. When an army is in the middle of a battle it is considered dangerous to lose focus. If you are distracted by the gun shots, bullets, and loud explosives you are not "war" ready. As a soldier, your position SHIFTS into becoming a liability if you are not strategically attentive to the assignment. To be quite frank, you become deadweight during a prayer assignment since you are mentally floating in the clouds. This is a form of dishonor to yourself, the team, and those who sacrificed their time to pray. While you are thinking about all of the things you need to do that day, your teammates will pay the price. Your teammates will be required to press to carry your portion in the spirit realm.

> *"For we do not wrestle against flesh and blood, but against principalities, against powers, against the rulers of the darkness of this age, against spiritual hosts of wickedness in the heavenly places"* (**Ephesians 6:12, New King James Version**).

Your "to-do" list becomes the very weapon that potentially causes the entire team to miss a miraculous move of God. We are seeking to take up ground in the heavenly places in prayer and intercession. While you are planning your day, the enemy is taking up ground. Do not become the intercessor that falls for the bait. You will open a door to unnecessary warfare that will drain prayer gatherings.

2. Social Media Entrapments

Social media plays a major role in the times we live in today. Technology will continue to evolve, whether we like it or not. Without second thought, thousands of people find themselves spending hours thoughtlessly scrolling social media applications. There are many who do not realize they have an addiction until they are told to fast from such activity. Social media becomes a distraction in prayer meetings when intercessors choose to disengage from prayer to scroll their timelines. You are subconsciously getting your needs met with something you deem "more entertaining" in that moment. I often found myself having the desire to pick up my phone to scroll when things become draining, unbearable, and somewhat boring during ministry and prayer events. We have all participated in at least one prayer meeting where the atmosphere felt exhausting. In those moments, you are more than likely sensing a plateau within the prayer gathering. You may be the intercessor God wants to utilize to SHIFT the prayers into a greater dimension. Social media will cause you to hide within meetings rather than being God's agent of change. You do not need the mic or platform to SHIFT atmospheres. As an intercessor, social media will cause you to shut yourself completely off from your surroundings. It is equivalent to sitting on a couch, turning on the television, and switching through movie channels. You are seeking to find something good to watch in the middle of prayer. Many of you may say, "Wow, it is not that deep" while reading this example. However, how many of you can account the events that transpired while you were scrolling? Social media can become a time-wasting tool that distracts intercessors from hearing or discerning the true voice of God in that moment.

3. **Texting/Frivolous Conversations**

> *"And this I say for your own profit, not that I may put a leash on you, but for what is proper, and that you may serve the Lord without distraction"* (**1Corinthians 7:35, New King James Version**).

Distractions can come in through friends, family members, and even those we are supposed to labor with. I have been in prayer meetings where there are frivolous conversations transpiring. This can happen through the form of texting as well. If you are holding a conversation that does not have anything to do with prayer, it should not be your priority in that moment. Unless it is an emergency, the conversation can wait. Distractions can come through bad decisions and the inadequate structure of our priorities. We must use wisdom when we are on assignment. When you call court into session, you are standing in the gap as God's chosen ambassador. You must serve without distraction.

4. Playing Favorites

When you are "playing favorites" you have identified who you find worthy of your undivided attention. You have mentally made a list of your favorite teammates/intercessors within your heart. This is a dangerous thing to do if you are not careful. You can quickly make someone an idol exalting them above the name of the Lord. Prayer warriors become prejudice against those who did not fit their standards of prayer. When you play favorites, you can easily zap out of the prayers. You can easily fall into the previous distraction entrapments while inviting the spirit of division. This is also a form of pride that will create a bigger issue within prayer teams if it is not dealt with. This is not to negate that there are some intercessors that are more advanced than others. It can take time to master the adequate skills to SHIFT people, atmosphere, lands, regions, and nations. Be careful not to step on those you should be esteeming greater than yourself. There is no such thing as a junior Holy Spirit. You should operate in excellence no matter who is leading the corporate prayer. We must remain intentional without conditions.

5. Falling into Tiredness

Tiredness becomes a distraction when you do not SHIFT into a place of towering over your emotions. Tiredness will cause prayer meetings to feel like a punishment, prison, or obligation. It SHIFTS you into a place of discontentment that causes your soul to speak louder than your spirit man. Your soul is self-conscious, while your spirit man is God-conscious. Have you ever participated in a gathering and wanted things to be "over already?" Tiredness causes negativity to override the systems of your thinking patterns. It will cause intercessors to become moody, snippy, unfiltered, and a potential agent of offense. Some seasons are harder than others where it requires a stronger pressing into the things of God. Tiredness is not always a demonic identification of spiritual warfare. Tiredness is a natural manifestation that stems from the lack of proper rest. If you are aware that you are tired, make the proper adjustments.

i.   Speak in fierce tongues to allow God to fill you. This allows you to operate in the strength of God. You dismantle your own strength while partnering with the Holy Spirit.

ii.   Walk around when you are undergirding your teammates. It is not wise to lay or slouch down when you are operating out of tiredness. This will keep you accountable from dosing off in corporate settings.

iii. Guarding your mouth and becoming a governor of your words. Many people become snippy, quick witted, or inconsolable when they are tired. Make sure to use wisdom in every interaction.   If you or a teammate fall into tiredness, stay a step ahead of the enemy by guarding your heart. Do not allow petty words or actions to remove you from your post.

iv.   Casting down false or vain imaginations. *"...casting down arguments and every high thing that exalts itself against the knowledge of God, bringing every thought into captivity to the obedience of Christ..."* **(2Corinthians 10:5, New King James Version)**. Do not give into blankly starring or daydreaming about what you could be doing in that moment. Cast down negative words, thoughts, and/or fantasies.

There is a plethora of distractions that we did not address. This is merely a tool to show you the power of distractions. Take the time to ask God what your personal distractions entail. Invite the Holy Spirit to reveal the open doors that cause you to take your eyes off of the assignment during prayer. SHIFT into becoming God's proficient marksman. You are God's skilled warrior!

Chapter 22

SHIFTING ATMOSPHERES VIA FINE ARTS MINISTRY

Fine arts ministry encompasses, psalmists, rappers, exhorters, minstrels, dancers, painters, poets, and those with creative abilities.

- Dance is the movement and embodiment of the word, presence, and purpose God.
- Song is the voice, melody, harmony, musicality, emotions, mind, and expressed ideas of the word, presence, and purpose of God.
- Music and Instruments are the sound, frequencies, radiance, rhythm, flavor, vibration, sovereign character and governmental authority of the word, presence, and purpose of God.
- Poetry and paintings reveal the creativity, visionary, heart, and clarity of the word, presence, and purpose of God.
- Dance materializes the physical manna of God.
- Song vocalizes the laws, standards, and nature of God.
- Music controls the airways with the infusion and rulership of the kingdom of God
- Poetry and paintings visually imprint and establish God's existence in the earth.

  2Corinthians 3:18 But we all, with open face beholding as in a glass the glory of the Lord, are changed into the same image from glory to glory, even as by the Spirit of the Lord.

Some atmospheres are not SHIFTED or sustained in the realms of God because the praise team leader, praise team, musicians and dance ministers do not know how to SHIFT atmospheres. Many (not all) of them do not know:

- God's voice and how to be guided by him in song, sound, and movement.
- Have not been taught how to SHIFT atmospheres in prayer thus being able to equate that revelation to song, sound, and movement.
- Do not know when an atmosphere is of God, hype, emotionalism, the devil, witchcraft, strange fire.
- How to use there calling to SHIFT darkness out and the kingdom of God in.
- Are prideful, not teachable as it relates the Lord's standards of gifts and callings, privileged due to superstardom of their gift, or ostracized due to their unique callings or personalities.
- Are gifted and talented but not anointed through relationship and covenant with God.
- Operate through gifts, talents and performance but not their callings.
- Do not know or are not taught the value of knowing the vision of a ministry or event they attend, or to seek God for his will so they have no understanding of governing, cultivating, or establishing a Godly atmosphere.
- Are paid for services rendered, and may not even attend the ministry, yet show up at rehearsals and on Sundays to lead worship.
- Have not been taught how to or the importance of working with the minister, prayer team, other fine arts teams to cultivate a kingdom atmosphere.
- Have not been grounded and branded fully in God and his authority and power, that even as they would attend secular events, they draw people out of darkness rather than succumb to mixture and strange fire, thus releasing that into Godly atmospheres.

Fine art ministers are frontliners for SHIFTING and governing atmospheres. They tend to be utilized to set the atmosphere for God's presence to rain and reign. If they are not provided the revelation and insights in this book, the body of Christ will continue to SHIFT and govern in measure. They must understand that this is part of their mantle and calling. That what they release invades the spiritual realms of God and SHIFTS what needs to be transferred with tangible manifestation into the earth realm.

Fine arts ministers need to be:

- Humble.
- Teachable.
- Trained not just in their gift but their calling.
- God rather than performance oriented.
- Equipped in embodying the word, presence, and kingdom of God.
- Keen in hearing, visualizing, seeing, sensing, discerning, knowing, producing, reproducing, God's voice, presence, and kingdom.
- Understand the vision for each service and the ministries they are partnering with.
- Able to seek God for their purpose of each service and ministries they are partnering with and equipped to bring it to pass with signs following.
- Open to working in unity with other fine arts ministers.
- Open to working in unity with the founder of the ministry, the minister or leader of each services, and with the ministers and prayers teams of each service.

Fine arts ministers must be discerning of what is going on in the people, the land, the atmosphere, and the heavenlies during services so they can continue to collaborate with the vision and the Holy Spirit to establish God's purpose and kingdom in that their midst and in the region.   They are not only able to pray but can use their creativity to confound demonic principalities and strongholds, break their powers, cast them out their darkness, while SHIFTING the light of God in. Decreeing Fine arts ministers will use the revelation in this book to equip themselves to SHIFT and govern Atmospheres. SHIFT!

Chapter 23

Exposing Prayer & Ministry Fillers

As we grow in prayer, utilizing our gifts, preaching and teaching, we want to be conscious of fillers.

Fillers are words we use in between sentences to connect our thoughts, or when we are thinking as we are presenting and conversing. It is okay that a few filler words slip out as this is a natural part of speaking. No one is going to think less of you if you say *"uhm"* *"like,* *"Lord God,"* *"Father God,"* once in a while. The goal is to avoid using fillers every three words or in every sentence.

We use filler words like *"um,"* *"like"* *"Lord God,"* *"Father God,"* because we are thinking or processing. Maybe we are searching for the right word, or we need to stop and formulate our next sentence. Often, we use them to indicate that we are going to talk, whether or not we have something to say at that very moment. Or to indicate that we are talking or praying to God.

We tend to use fillers due to:

Habit - They become a part of our prayer life or teaching lifestyle.

Religion - It is with the culture of our ministry so now we engage in it. Or it is religious to say, *"Lord God"* and so as we pray, etc., we have started to engage in this religious pattern.

Internal Anxiety - We are experiencing this within ourselves as we pray. Therefore, the spirit of fear, nervousness, timidity, and anxiety needs to be cleansed in our soul and heart.

Unconscious Insecurity - We have some insecurity issues within our heart and soul so they subtly manifest in our prayer lives and ministry teachings.

Splits or Damage to the Brain - There may be area of the brain that is damaged, split, or fragmented, so it causes us to be a bit scattered when we talk, pray, or publicly speak.

- Pray for healing of damaged areas of your brain, especially as it relates to your memory, memory recall, and intellect.
- Break the powers and triggers of memory recall where traumas, unresolved issues, hurts, pains, revert you back to old issues, thoughts, desires, habits, and behaviors.
- The brain is also divided into several lobes that must function properly for the brain to work properly. Decree healing over these lobes:
  - The frontal lobe is responsible for problem solving, judgment and motor function.
  - The parietal lobe manages sensation, handwriting, and body position.
  - The temporal lobes are involved with memory and hearing.
  - The occipital lobe contains the brain's visual processing system.
  - The brain is surrounded by a layer of tissue called the meninges. The skull (cranium) helps protect the brain from injury.
- Break the power of witchcraft spells, death and dumb spirits, brain fog, confusion, psychic powers, telepathy, psychological and emotional warfare, and word curses that may be binding the brain.
- Cleanse out little girl and little boy spirits that may be lodged in the brain or soul. These are arrested

development spirits lodged in areas of your brain and soul when traumatic past issues have occurred to stunt full growth; or when parts of your identity or personally have not matured to your full age.

- Command all personality splits to be healed and deal with any underlying issues to them.
- Cleanse out negativity, thought racing, stress, wavering, doublemindedness, unbelief, low self-esteem, and low self-worth, that may plague the thought life.

Lack of Expanded Spiritual Vocabulary – An expanded spiritual vocabulary is needed so that we tap into more words that relate to what we are praying for or teaching. Study power scriptures related to the prayer assignments and requests you are taking before the Lord. Use the dictionary to expand your vocabulary of words as this will broaden your revelation and creativity to tower and SHIFT through prayer realms without stuttering, filtering, questioning, or fearing.

Chapter 24

Cleansing Prayer & Ministry Fillers

Receive deliverance and healing from the spirit of fear (e.g. Fear of public speaking, fear of failing, messing up, not being good enough; anxiety, panic attacks, stress whether knowingly or unknowingly causes fear, fright and intimidation of people or to minister in front of people).

Receive deliverance and healing of insecurities and identity issues (e.g. Not feeling good enough or worthy, comparing self to others, unconsciously or consciously competing with others or to be the best rather than resting in God to simply use you, having perfectionist qualities, having to be the best).

Practice praying out loud in your private prayer time. When preparing for a prayer assignment, sermon or teaching, practice reciting it out loud rather reviewing it silently. The more you hear yourself say it the more you become it.

Study vocabulary words on the characteristics of God, names of God, and descriptions of God, so they will flow out of your spirit when you are praying and teaching. Study these from the bible but also explore words in general that describe God and then look them up in the dictionary and study the meanings and synonyms of those words.

Study scripture and practice reciting and declaring scriptures out loud.

Study scripture and practice praying into that scripture or those passages of scripture. Study the Hebrew and Greek meanings behind words in that scripture. Study that scripture in different versions of the bible. Then pray a prayer using those different versions and meanings as you pray into that scripture.

Write your own prayers, then pray them out loud during your prayer time.

Practice praying in your prayer language. Pray in tongues at least 30 minutes to an hour daily then spend at least ten minutes waiting on God to speak. Journal what he says. Focus on the Holy Spirit while praying in tongues and seeking him for revelation of what you are praying. Practice surrendering your will, mouth, and tongue, while being led by the Holy Spirit via prayer. This postures you inside your prayer language and enables you to exercise your spiritual eyes, ears, senses, discernment, judgment, and knowing (faith) of God as you pray. The more you rely on the Holy Spirit to guide and lead you in prayer, the less likely you are to experience soul challenges or mind issues, where fillers surface while you pray.

Seek God in healing and making you bold in your identity and calling. Learn to relax in who you are and live fierce in your uniqueness. Relax in your ability to pray and minister through the Holy Ghost. Though you want to be mindful of timing and time allotted to you, do not rush or feel the need to rush your prayer or teaching. Trust that if you have been called upon to minister, then you will do it through God's timing and efficiency.

Be okay with pausing to gather your thoughts or a focus of the point you are considering at that moment; take a moment for others to absorb what you are praying and teaching.

Slow down as going too fast can cause you to become tongue-tied. It is also what causes the brain to get ahead of our spirit which can trigger a filler.

Go back and listen to the recordings of your prayers and teaching. Or record yourself on your phone app and listen to them. Identify the fillers you use and journal them. Search out the underlying reasons for your fillers and when you most often use them. Deal with any underlying issues God may reveal to you while you are listening. Explore what was occurring in you when you used certain fillers and then practice weeding those things out of your speech and communication patterns. This will diminish your use of fillers.

Continue practicing these steps until they become a part of your ministry lifestyle where you have lessened your use of fillers and are flowing more powerfully in the strength and grace of the Lord when praying, teaching, preaching and communicating.

Chapter 25

Demonic Interference or Attacks

This is a list of spirits that attack people, prayers, equipment, and communications, during events, times of prayer, and within a prayer team.

Leviathan - Interrupts and distorts communication between the speaker and the listener.

Radan – Spirit that interrupts, distorts, damages, and prevents the proper working of technology to frustrate and steal your focus when praying or speaking.

Python – Wraps itself around a person, place, or thing. Restricts, squeezes, and suffocates thoughts, words, and information. The person may start to cough and choke, the sound may become very tight in a person, speakers, or device and the sound may go in and out.

Mind Binding & Mind Blinding Spirits – Can look like a squid or octopus sitting on the head with its tentacles pressed into the eyes, forehead, nose, ears, temples, back of the head, neck, and scull. Binds and blinds the mind and senses so you cannot operate effectively. May feel like pressure, migraine, or tormenting headache, or as if something is sticking you in the eyes and ears. The spirit realm and vision may look black, dark, empty, foggy, and cloudy. You may become dull of hearing because of a clogging of the ears and temples, and you may feel like something is sitting on your head or wrapped around your head.

Death & Dumb Spirit - Causes stuttering, loss of words, discombobulation, scattering in the thought processing or words, inability to discern what God is wanting you to say or do, dullness in thought or hearing, slowness in one's intellect or ability to learn or flow in their gifting, flow in prayer, etc. Sometime the person, team, or congregation appears unusually still as if they are not in the room even though they are physically present, or as if they are watching a movie even though they are supposed to be engaged in the task at hand.

Witchcraft Words & Spells – This is sent from witches and warlocks, demonic people, or from friendly fire. It filters into the speech of a person to hinder the prayers and words from being clear and effective. Its ultimate purpose is to bring confusion and mixture.

Spirits of Confusion – Causes disorientation, frustration, incoherence, forgetfulness, puzzling, baffling, mixed emotions, mix up in communication between those praying and regarding assignments. Can work together with the death and dumb spirit, witchcraft and mind blinding spirits.

Zapping Spirit – Steals information by zapping your words from the brain as you pray and teach.

Competition & Performance – Can cause impure motives, strife, pride, haughtiness, contention, jealousy, ambition, false sense of security, idolatry to override the prayer focus. It will feel like the person literally exalted themselves above God, the prayer assignment, and their motives will fill up the atmosphere.

Spirit of Apathy – Can quench the Holy Spirit and the SHIFT of God due to the absence of passion, emotion, excitement, zeal or faith to pray, to press in to prayer, to support others as they pray, or to see prayers come to past. Though physically present, there is a lack of concern, desire, drive, or conviction for the prayer assignment or pressing into the fullness of God.

Spirit of Listlessness – There is a lack of discipline to pray with fervor. The person tends to be idle, passive, dull, lazy; the person may become tired, disinterested, inattentive, unenergetic when it is time to pray. This spirit tends to work with python.

Spirit of Slothfulness – A spirit of stupor, slumber, lethargy, passivity, sluggardness, and pressing heaviness, binds the person or atmosphere. The demon loathes the person or atmosphere to sleep, or makes them so slow that they appear sleep.

Chapter 26

Identifying Words of the Lord

Just because a word of revelation from God is spoken does not mean it is a prophecy. Prophecy, exhortation, the word of knowledge, the word of wisdom, tongues, interpretations of tongues and other verbal forms of edification are all vocal gifts. However, they are very distinct and separate operations of the Holy Spirit. To say every spoken word is "prophecy" is simply wrong.

It is important to know what type of word you are receiving from God and giving to the receiver so the word can be applied and governed appropriately. This diminishes error with mishandling the word and with having expectations or perceptions of the word that God did not state. For this reason, I teach my team the types of words God provides, and encourage them to share what type of word it is when they are releasing it to others (*Study 1Corinthians 12 and Isaiah 11*).

Prophecy - Edify, comfort, and exhort a person or body of people; testifies of the goodness of Jesus. Though the releaser may provide past and present knowledge, the prophecy provides foresight into the future. If there is no foresight, it is not a prophecy. If a person is in the office of a prophet, they can judge, rebuke, correct, direct, and display the anger of the Lord to a people, region, or nation.

Prophecy in the Greek is ***prophēteia*** and means "*prediction (scriptural or other), a discourse emanating from divine inspiration and declaring the purposes of God, whether by reproving and admonishing the wicked, or comforting the afflicted, or revealing things hidden; esp. by foretelling future events.*"

Exhortation, Edification, Encouragement - An utterance, discourse, declaration, poem, affirmation, conversation, address, speech, prayer, teaching, conveying motivation, invitation, comfort, encouragement, strength, love, mercy, goodness, faithfulness, and spiritual help that SHIFT a person or atmosphere into the presence, focus, and purpose of God. A person with this gift operates through the sovereignty of God. They are clear and unwavering about his character and nature and are able to empower people to trust his sovereignty (*Acts 11:23-24, Acts 14:21-22, Acts 15:32, Romans 12:7-8, Romans 14:19 Romans 15:2, John 14:16, 2Timothy 4:2, 1Thessalonians 5:11*).

Exhortation in Greek *is **parakaléō*** meaning to properly, *"to call near, invite, invoke, intreat, make a call, summons, to encourage, urge, comfort, strengthen, or receive consolation."* Refers to believers offering up evidence that stands up in God's court where God's judgement and justice is used to empower a person, place, situation, or thing.

Edification in Greek is ***oikodomé*** which is *"the act of building, a building, spiritual advancement, edification or upbuilding."* A person is actually operating as a divine architecture to build a structure whether that be a person, place, or thing. It is the divine ability to promote growth in Godly wisdom, quality, honor, holiness, equity, joy, and fulfillment.

Encouragement in Greek is ***paráklēsis*** and *"it is an intimate call that someone personally gives to deliver God's verdict, the close-call that reveals how the Lord weighs in the relevant facts (evidence)."* It is a *"holy urging"* of the Lord directly motivating, empowering, supporting, prompting, and inspiring believers to carry out his plan and purpose in their lives and spheres of influence.

Knowledge- Facts, information, understanding, or the state of being aware of something about a person or situation via the

Holy Spirit. One with this gift can also exemplify knowledge beyond their years or natural understanding. They have no means of proving what they know other than by the Holy Spirit and the confirmation of others. When they study information, they receive increased knowledge from the Holy Spirit even though they do not have the education or expertise for what they know. Such persons may also bring forth, report, make known, give facts, pass on, convey awareness, have insight, understanding, and intelligence via the Holy Spirit. What they share is intended to draw the person into trusting God and posturing them in a place of receiving deliverance, healing, prophecy, and instruction to further advance their lives or situations through the purpose of God.

Knowledge in Greek is ***gnósis*** meaning *"knowledge, science, doctrine, intelligence, or divine understanding."* It is the knowledge of God offered to advance the gospel through what has been conveyed.

Wisdom - The natural and/or spirit ability to understand things that other people cannot understand or do not have the knowledge of. They possess a perspective of what is proper, reasonable, good sense or balanced judgment. Those with the gift of wisdom have the experience, gift of common sense, enlightenment, clear thinking, foresight, perception, brains, sanity, or stability of God released to enlighten, empower, and advance people, situations, lands, atmospheres, and regions.

The wisdom of God actually has a personality. *James 3:17* contends that *"But the wisdom that is from above is first pure, then peaceable, gentle, and easy to be intreated, full of mercy and good fruits, without partiality, and without hypocrisy."*

Wisdom in the Greek is ***sophia*** and means *"broad and full of intelligence, the intimate understanding of God's word and purpose."*

Proverbs 4:7 Wisdom is the principal thing; therefore get wisdom: and with all thy getting get understanding.

The word principal means chief, first, first fruits, order, rank, beginning. It is essential to receive wisdom from God before making any decisions and putting any actions in motion. Wisdom in the Hebrews is *hakma*, meaning skillful. It means skillful in:

1. War
2. Administration of wisdom
3. Religious affairs
4. Ethical matters

Wisdom enables a person to skillfully implement the will, intent, and purposes of God. People can receive advice but if that insight does not reveal skill that enables a person to understand and activate what God is saying, then it is not God's wisdom.

Counsel – Insight that breathes life, instruction, exploration, direction, strategy, support, encouragement, and focus, into a person or situation to help process and progress them or that matter towards the destined purpose in God.

Counsel in Greek is **sumboulion** which is defined as *"a body of advisers (assessors) in a court, a council, consultation, counsel, advice; resolution, decree."*

Counseling is not advice. It is a committed processing to wholeness. The counselor or releaser of the word is not responsible for the healing, but is responsible for making themselves available to the healing process. Words of counsel provides enlightenment and instruction of how to journey with God to a specific point of wellness. This counsel can have a prophetic element to a future destination but the instruction and exploration itself is not prophecy. It is the counsel of the Lord.

Understanding - To perceive the meaning of, grasp the idea of, comprehend, connect the insights, or provide clarity to what God is speaking or what is being revealed. Understanding means to assign a meaning to, interpret; to comprehend the significance or importance of, to learn, perceive, hear, accept as true, trust or believe. It also means to embrace, partner with or grab hold to a thirst for knowledge, discern, sense, recognize, make sense of, fathom, or take in the truth, will, intent, and purpose of the wisdom and revelation that is being given.

Understand in Hebrew is **binah** meaning *"knowledge, wisdom, meaning, perfectly, understanding, discernment, and truth."*

Speaking in Tongues (*1Corinthians 14:4-5*) – Is the literal dialect and prayer language between you and God given to you by the Holy Spirit. Speaking in tongues is a real language. It is the voice of God speaking through you in different languages that he desires to impart into your life.

Tongues in Greek is **glóssa** meaning *"a language that is not naturally acquired; a tongue, used of flowing speech, verbal utterance, speaking that is inspired by God."*

Interpretation of Tongues - Being able to translate what God is saying and speaking from one language to another where the people are able to understand his revelation, knowledge, word, counsel, strategy, guidance, and instruction. This gift tends to be released when there are prophetic words and prayer going forth. Someone may speak in tongues and SHIFT from speaking in tongues to praying or prophesying what the Lord is wanting to be said or desire to be released at that time. Some may also speak in tongues and another person/s may interpret what is said.

Strategy – A buzz word we tend to hear in this day and age is *"strategy."* We have come to recognize that as God speaks, we also need strategy to implement what he is saying. This is good because God's words tend to be progressive and requires movement and work along with faith to manifest them.

> **John 2:26** *For as the body without the spirit is dead, so faith without works is dead also.*

Even if we are standing in faith, it requires energy, focus, and active contending to remain grounded in what God has said. This in and of itself may require strategy so that we do not give into unbelief, ungodly voices, or fatigue. We may need to be careful of being in certain places, being around certain people, remain fervent in fasting and praying, and building ourselves up in a particular characteristic in God so we will not get sifted by the enemy or unholy alliances. Thus infers strategy.

Dictionary.com defines *strategy* as, *"the science or art of combining and employing the means of war in planning and directing large military movements and operations."* It is *"a plan, method, or series of maneuvers or stratagems for obtaining a specific goal or result."*

A strategy can include words of exhortation, wisdom, revelation, knowledge, counsel, and understanding. All of these can be part of your strategy. A strategy is your war plan that keeps us fortified as we walk out the words of God. Once you have the strategy, then you implement tactics necessary to SHIFT forward in unveiling the word God has given you.

Offensive against attacks	Grounded
Rooted	Focused
Seated in heavenly places of authority	Towering over trials & obstacles

Strategy Provides:

Shelter	Protection
Trust	Hope
Fortress	Defense
Deliverance	Rescue
Recovery	Healing
Peace despite war	Rest from war
Safety for harvest & spoils of war	Set altar of worship

Strategy helps you to resist being worried, fearful, inferior, or insecure as you know God's got you. He has given you a plan to keep you solidified in his secret place. You can work your strategy to remain fortified as God works his word for and in you. You do not change the strategy unless God leads. I seek God for strategy as weeks, months, and seasons change so I will know how to further progress in a word or vision that God has given me. I do this because what may have worked last week or month may not work for this week or month. I may be facing different devils, trials, obstacles and require a different strategy. I will only know that by seeking God for that revelation. I implement what God says and if he does not give me anything, then I continue to work the current strategy he has provided.

Study Exploration
1. As God releases words to you, identify with him what type of word it is. Make sure you label it as such when

journaling it or when sharing it with others. The more you identify your well, the more mature you will become in knowing how God speaks, hearing him, and being able to convey his word to others.

2. As God would release words, seek him for a strategy for how to stand and birth forth what he is speaking. Do not sway from the strategy unless he releases another strategy. When you find yourself fearful, weary, or stressed, check your strategy to make sure you are implementing it properly. Sometimes we are not implementing the full strategy and it can cause sifting or unnecessary warfare. God may tell you to declare the prophetic word out loud three times a day for a week and too fast and pray until 5pm. You may fast and pray but not declare three times a day and thus ensue sifting and warfare. You may think this part is unnecessary, forget to do it, or just lax. But when reassessing your strategy you will remember to implement this part and it will stop the sifting and unnecessary warfare. So always go back and reassess and do everything God is requiring, even those things you may think are meaningless. God uses the foolish things to confound the wise. Be mindful of that and know your strategy has power to fortify you against the enemy.

> **2Corinthians 1:27** *But God hath chosen the foolish things of the world to confound the wise; and God hath chosen the weak things of the world to confound the things which are mighty.*
>
> **2Corinthians 10:4** *For the weapons of our warfare are not carnal, but mighty through God to the pulling down of strong holds.* **SHIFT!**

Chapter 27

Ordained Identity Declaration

Jesus, I decree that I am your (decree who you are – i.e., apostle, prophet, teacher, evangelist, pastor, minister, proclaimer of the gospel)!

I break every curse against my identity in the name of Jesus! For I am what I am by the grace of God.

I am your dreamer that provokes others to dream again, a birther of manifestation in the earth!

I am your chain breaker, your deliverer, your stealth bomber, your weapon of mass destruction!

I am manifold grace and glory, kingdom armory overflowing with kingdom keys, be though made whole, and euodoo prosperity!

I am soar prophetic, praise party, a leader to leaders, and mentor to mentees!

I am your revivalist, your reformer, your strategist, your solution to the body of Christ and to the world.

I am your scout, your gatekeeper, your watchdog, your watchman, that lives and rules in spiritual realms, while governing my God ordained regions and spheres of influence!

I am your dismantler and displacer of demonic strongholds, territorial spirits, and principalities!

I am your judge of witches, warlocks, demonic powers, idolatry, and wickedness on earth and in high places!

I am your pioneer, your trailblazer, your business owner, your marketplace infiltrator!

I am your vision carrier, your glory carrier, your praiser, your worshipper, your servant!

I am your friend, your pen, your scribe, your author, your word made manifest in the earth!

I am fusion - fused with heavenly council and authority to reign internationally in the earth. I am your hybrid believer, your disruptor causing disruptions and an overthrowing of demonic systems and kingdoms!

I am your KINGDOM SHIFTER! A SHIFTER - mandated to raise up other KINGDOM SHIFTERS for your glory. I do not apologize that my very identity SHIFTS people, situations, lands, atmospheres, climates, and regions.

For through you Jesus, I have permission to be me. I am one of many faces, mantles, and giftings, yet I walk in my true God given identity. There is no one else I would rather be. I am who you ordained me to be.

Chapter 28

Dominion and Authority Decree

I decree I am eternally surrounded and consumed inside the glory and consuming fire of the Lord.

I decree I eternally operate in the revival streams of dominion and authority. I am eternally seated inside of Christ in the third heavens and only go higher and deeper in the realms of your apostolic authority, revival fire, and dominion glory. I saturate and cultivate myself in your authority and dominion and decree it is the consumption of my destiny and calling.

I honor God with my whole life - with my whole heart, my whole mind, my whole soul. Nothing but honor will you receive from me.

I decree the eternal favor and blessings of heaven is the truth, will, purpose, glory and honor around me and all that concerns me.

Because of the operations of the kingdom of heaven in my life, I am honored by God and man! I cannot be denied for the kingdom of God works in my life, for my life, through my life, and is the atmosphere and governmental rule of me and everything which concerns me.

I decree the DUNAMIS and EXOUSIA power and authority of the Lord is eternally upon me to heal the sick, raise the dead, cast out devils, cleanse the leopards, and to freely give as I have received.

I decree the EXOUSIA power of God gives me the ability, capability, privilege, authority, right, and enablement to successfully advance in my life's vision and destiny.

I decree I sow myself - my life is a seed. I sow in financial giving and through all God desires me to release. I want for nothing because God is my provider; my seeds also produce overflowing harvest that takes care of all that concerns me and what God has granted unto me.

I decree an unwavering spirit of belief, faith and kingdom authority is mantled upon me to produce immediate, sustaining, limitless miracles, signs, wonders, deliverance, healing, cures, and breakthrough, as I am a tangible witness that God is the only savior and reigning king.

SHIFT AGAIN!
I decree a DEMONSTRATIVE warfare mantle is upon me where I have:

- Power over all the power of the enemy and nothing by any means harms me.
- Power to tower in victory and dominion over every principality, power, ruler of darkness, territorial spirit, ruler in high places, witches, warlocks, curses, ungodly plots, plans, assignments, and challenging situations.
- Power to cast out every strongman and devil and dismantle and annihilate to utter destruction every demonic kingdom, webbing, trap, troop, force field, barrier, and fortress I encounter.
- Power to heal every manner of sickness, affliction, transgression, disease, and distress.
- Power to SHIFT every person, atmosphere, region that I encounter into the glory, judgment, grace, salvation, likeness, kingdom, and will of God.

SHIFT AGAIN!

I decree the power gifts from *1Corinthians 12* are tangibly and consistently operating in my life. I decree supernatural DUNAMIS and EXOUSIA power of the Holy Spirit operates immeasurably in me through the gifts of the Holy Spirit. I decree the:

1. Word of Wisdom
2. Word of Knowledge
3. Supernatural Gift of Faith
4. Gifts of Extraordinary Healing
5. Working of Miracles
6. Gift of Prophecy
7. Discerning of Spirits
8. Divers (or different) kinds of Tongues
9. Interpretation of (different) Tongues
10. Spirit of Empowerment, Proclamation & Exhortation
11. Gifts of Helps & Hospitality

Operates in me with limitless evidence and unlimited measure in the name of Jesus.

I Decree The Seven Fold Spirit Of God From *Isaiah 11:2* Is Upon Me!

I decree the Spirit of the Lord is the supernatural power source that creates God's thoughts and purposes in my mind and heart, and produces God's will and plan in my life and sphere of influence.

I decree the Spirit of Wisdom is God's supernatural thoughts, insight, and scholarly knowledge mantling and becoming me - operating in me and through me.

I decree the Spirit of Understanding is God's personal illumination, enlightenment and revelation guiding me and

186

my life's vision; and leading me to guide the purposes, plans, and destinies of others.

I decree the Spirit of Counsel is God's personal instructions and guidance delivering and healing me and enabling me to freely deliver, heal, and empower the lives of others.

I decree the Spirit of Strength & Supernatural Power is God's supernatural endowment vested upon me to perform his thoughts, will, plan, and miracles in my life, ministry, life endeavors, and destiny.

I decree the Spirit of Knowledge quickens and provokes God's intellect and truth to full manifestation in my life, actions, abilities, situations, ministries, ministry activities, businesses, and endeavors.

I decree the Fear of the Lord is in me towering in God's love, reverence and truth, while enabling me to resist anything that would quench His Spirit in and through me. I am unquenchable through the fear of the Lord, and greater works than Jesus I do, as I do only what I see and hear my father in heaven do, and leads me to do through my friend the Holy Spirit as I govern and SHIFT atmospheres here in the earth.

Daily, I live grounded from the kingdom of heaven and from a kingdom mindset and stance in the name of Jesus.

Daily I live inside the disruptive SHIFT realm and momentum of God.

I am not afraid to DISRUPT AND SHIFT and journey through the impetus timing and purpose of God. For we are in covenant and this is my inherited portion as a son/daughter, an heir to the kingdom of heaven.

So Jesus! I unwaveringly declare that I tower in your revealed grace, glory, love, and power from now and forevermore! It is so! AMEN!

Chapter 29

Prayer That Sets Atmospheres

Our Father which art in heaven, Hallowed be thy name.
Lord you are awesome. You are wonderful. You are great.
You are grand. You are matchless. You are sovereign. Lord
you are governor. You are the government. You are the law.
You have all autonomy - you are a self-government, who can
rule you? You have unlimited power. You have uninhibited
authority. You have all dominion. You are the ultimate truth.

*Thy kingdom come, Thy will be done in earth, as it is in
heaven.*

As we declare your sovereign rule, we break open heaven
with your triumphant name and command a SHIFT right now
from heaven to earth. We say heavens open as we blast
through every brass ceiling and hammer through every
demonic fortress. We command the heavens to open wide
and spread all over our region. We call forth angels to come
and keep the heavens open so we can have full access to our
Lord and savior Jesus and his kingdom. We decree the blood
of Jesus, the fire of God and the glory of God around our
region and declare it belongs to Jesus and Jesus only. We
close up every demonic portal and seal off any entryways that
are not God's gates to our region. We SHIFT to our rightful
place into the third heavens and stand victoriously at the
gates. We declare we are the gatekeepers and assert our right
to govern our land and sphere.

We command the atmosphere to be endued with heaven - to
take on the tangible fruit, blessings, wellness, aroma, and
manifestation of heaven. We call forth angels to come and
contend with any demonic forces that would contend against
us. We declare principalities, territorial spirits and powers are

bound as angels join forces to assert your government and rule. We thank you oh angels of the Lord for ministering with us and aiding us in governing every sphere and realm under our heavenlies. May a scattering and displacement occur against all darkness, all manner of evil, all powers, and spiritual wickedness in high places. May judgment break the backs of enemies that defy God and defy our works on his behalf. Decreeing judgment and annihilation of their workings even now. Decreeing judgement and death to every witch and warlock in our sphere that will not bow, turn and serve Jesus. Decreeing a bowing and a surrendering to our only Lord and savior Jesus.

Give us this day our daily bread.

We thank you that your kingdom is now Jesus. We thank you that it is at hand. We feast off the goodness of your kingdom even now. We feast on your manna from heaven. May your word feed us from the goodness of your hand and the strength of your grace. May your word feed the atmosphere with your love and power. We soak the atmosphere with the breath of your glory even now. We say breathe God and eat on the goodness of his love. Breathe glory and feast on the goodness of his glory. We command an unveiling of the glory of God that was instilled in the earth from the beginning of time. Reveal yourself, enmesh with heaven, and manifest the tangible fruit of heaven in our midst. Oh Lord, we declare that you are good as we partake of you. Oh Lord we declare that you are delicious, as we consume of you.

And forgive us our debts, as we forgive our debtors.

Even as we feast on you, we repent for every sin seen and unseen. We repent for everything we have partaken of that is not of you. We repent to feasting at your table then feasting at the table of devils. We repent personally, generationally, regionally, on behalf of the body of Christ, and our nation. We repent for every open door to demons, all witchcraft and idolatry, sacrifices to demonic altars knowingly and unknowingly, and ungodly blood shed upon our land and in the land of our region. We loose the blood of Jesus to cleanse ourselves, our atmosphere, our land, the frequencies and airways, the climate, people, realms and spheres of our region. We soak ourselves and our region in your precious blood and thank you for the redemption power that purifies and transforms us.

And lead us not into temptation, but deliver us from evil.

We declare no temptation as we resist all evil. Even now we declare deliverance from any evil and all demons. We renounce the devil and all his ways and command a binding and casting out of every spirit that is not like you. We bind up all squatter and watcher spirits in and around our land. We bind them with fetters and chains, and cast them out of our sphere in the name of Jesus. We loose confusion to all demonic agents on assignment against our lives, ministries, businesses, and events. We command a confusion and a confounding to them even now. Let them stumble back to their camp in such disarray that they attack their own camp – causing a fury where they take one another out. We loose bombs of fire and hailstone into camps and high places that would prey and loose spells and contention against us. Angels of the living God go into those places and further burn those camps and high places down and further destroy all that is attached to them. We decree this is the day of total deliverance. We rejoice and declare deliverance on every side. We rejoice and ask for more infusing of the kingdom of heaven, drenching of the Holy Spirit and declare deliverance in the name of Jesus.

For thine is the kingdom, and the power, and the glory,
forever. Amen.

For thine is your kingdom God – the power and the glory. We declare an infusion of your power and glory into the atmosphere. We declare your demonstrative power with manifestations of miracles, signs, and wonders following. We well up in your power even now. We say the land, frequencies and heavens are welling up with your power and glory right now. We speak into your glory and declare the laws of heaven – the purpose of heaven is solidifying this prayer. We thank you for answering our prayer and for the immediate fruit that is and will continue to manifest from this prayer. It is so in Jesus name. **SHIFT!** Amen!

BOOK REFERENCES

➢ *Blueletterbible.com*

➢ *Biblestudytools.com*

➢ *Dictionary.com*

➢ *Dry land image is from https://yessweeterthanhoney.wordpress.com/2012/07/13/thirst-for-the-lord-today/*

➢ *Olivetree.com*

➢ *Circle of Incantations Picture is from https://www.tumblr.com/search/circles%20of%20incantations*

➢ *Strong's Exhaustive Bible Concordance Online Bible Study Tools*

➢ *The Great Awakening: Igniting Regional Revival by Taquetta Baker*

➢ *Wikipedia*

❖ *Front Book cover photo by Tashema Davis. Connect with her via Facebook.*
❖ *Cover photo by Reenita Keys. Connect with her via Facebook.*

❖ *Editing by Amanda Latrice. Connect with her via Facebook.*

Kingdom Shifters Books & Apparel

Available at <u>Kingdomshifters.com</u>

BOOKS FOR EVERYONE

Healing The Wounded Leader
Kingdom Shifters Decree That Thang
There Is An App For That
Kingdom Watchman Builder On The Wall
Embodiment Of A Kingdom Watchman
Dismantling Homosexuality Handbook
Release The Vision
Feasting In His Presence
Kingdom Heirs Decree That Thang

Let There Be Sight
Atmosphere Changers (Weaponry)
Apostolic Governing
Apostolic Mantle
Dance From Heaven To Earth
Annihilating Church Hurt
Discerning The Voice of God
Birthing Books That Shifts Generations
Prayers That Shift Atmospheres

BOOKS FOR DANCERS
Dancers! Dancers! Dancers! Decree That Thang
Spirits That Attack Dance Ministers & Ministries
Dance & Fivefold Ministry
Dance From Heaven To Earth

CD'S
Decree That Thang CD
Kingdom Heirs Decree That Thang CD
Teaching & Worship CD's

www.ingramcontent.com/pod-product-compliance
Lightning Source LLC
LaVergne TN
LVHW091253080426
835510LV00007B/238